# MAD LIBS®

# HOLLY, JOLLY MAD LIBS

By Roger Price and Leonard Stern

MAD LIBS

An Imprint of Penguin Random House LLC

Mad Libs format and text copyright © 2009, 2007, 2005, 2003, 2001, 1985 by Penguin Random House LLC.
All rights reserved.

Concept created by Roger Price & Leonard Stern

*Holly, Jolly Mad Libs* published in 2009 by Price Stern Sloan.
This edition published in 2017 by Mad Libs,
an imprint of Penguin Random House LLC, New York.
Printed in the USA.

Visit us online at penguinrandomhouse.com

*Holly, Jolly Mad Libs* ISBN 9780843189506
19 20 18

# MAD LIBS®

# INSTRUCTIONS

MAD LIBS® is a game for people who don't like games!
It can be played by one, two, three, four, or forty.

## ● RIDICULOUSLY SIMPLE DIRECTIONS

In this tablet you will find stories containing blank spaces where words are left out. One player, the READER, selects one of these stories. The READER does not tell anyone what the story is about. Instead, he/she asks the other players, the WRITERS, to give him/her words. These words are used to fill in the blank spaces in the story.

## ● TO PLAY

The READER asks each WRITER in turn to call out a word—an adjective or a noun or whatever the space calls for—and uses them to fill in the blank spaces in the story. The result is a MAD LIBS® game.

When the READER then reads the completed MAD LIBS® game to the other players, they will discover that they have written a story that is fantastic, screamingly funny, shocking, silly, crazy, or just plain dumb—depending upon which words each WRITER called out.

## ● EXAMPLE (*Before* and *After*)

"_____!" he said _____
    EXCLAMATION               ADVERB

as he jumped into his convertible _____ and
                                       NOUN

drove off with his _____ wife.
                   ADJECTIVE

"*Ouch*_____!" he said *Stupidly*_____
    EXCLAMATION               ADVERB

as he jumped into his convertible *cat*_____ and
                                       NOUN

drove off with his *brave*_____ wife.
                   ADJECTIVE

# MAD LIBS®

# QUICK REVIEW

In case you have forgotten what adjectives, adverbs, nouns, and verbs are, here is a quick review:

An **ADJECTIVE** describes something or somebody. *Lumpy, soft, ugly, messy,* and *short* are adjectives.

An **ADVERB** tells how something is done. It modifies a verb and usually ends in "ly." *Modestly, stupidly, greedily,* and *carefully* are adverbs.

A **NOUN** is the name of a person, place, or thing. *Sidewalk, umbrella, bridle, bathtub,* and *nose* are nouns.

A **VERB** is an action word. *Run, pitch, jump,* and *swim* are verbs. Put the verbs in past tense if the directions say PAST TENSE. *Ran, pitched, jumped,* and *swam* are verbs in the past tense.

When we ask for **A PLACE**, we mean any sort of place: a country or city *(Spain, Cleveland)* or a room *(bathroom, kitchen)*.

An **EXCLAMATION** or **SILLY WORD** is any sort of funny sound, gasp, grunt, or outcry, like *Wow!, Ouch!, Whomp!, Ick!,* and *Gadzooks!*

When we ask for specific words, like a **NUMBER**, a **COLOR**, an **ANIMAL**, or a **PART OF THE BODY**, we mean a word that is one of those things, like *seven, blue, horse,* or *head*.

When we ask for a **PLURAL**, it means more than one. For example, *cat* pluralized is *cats*.

# MAD LIBS®

## CHRISTMAS CAROL MAD LIBS

MAD LIBS® is fun to play with friends, but you can also play it by yourself! To begin with, DO NOT look at the story on the page below. Fill in the blanks on this page with the words called for. Then, using the words you have selected, fill in the blank spaces in the story.

Now you've created your own hilarious MAD LIBS® game!

# JINGLE BELLS

PLURAL NOUN _____

ANIMAL _____

NOUN _____

PLURAL NOUN _____

VERB ENDING IN "ING" _____

PLURAL NOUN _____

PLURAL NOUN _____

VERB _____

PLURAL NOUN _____

PLURAL NOUN _____

VERB _____

ANIMAL _____

# MAD LIBS®
## JINGLE BELLS

Dashing through the _____
                                PLURAL NOUN

In a one-_____ open _____,
               ANIMAL                       NOUN

O'er the _____ we go,
              PLURAL NOUN

_____ all the way.
  VERB ENDING IN "ING"

_____ on bobtails ring,
  PLURAL NOUN

Making _____ bright.
        PLURAL NOUN

What fun it is to _____ and sing
                  VERB

A sleighing song tonight!

Jingle _____, jingle _____,
      PLURAL NOUN               PLURAL NOUN

Jingle all the way!

Oh, what fun it is to _____
                    VERB

In a one-_____ open sleigh.
         ANIMAL

MAD LIBS® is fun to play with friends, but you can also play it by yourself! To begin with, DO NOT look at the story on the page below. Fill in the blanks on this page with the words called for. Then, using the words you have selected, fill in the blank spaces in the story.

Now you've created your own hilarious MAD LIBS® game!

## GOING CAROLING

ADJECTIVE _____

ADJECTIVE _____

NUMBER _____

ADJECTIVE _____

PLURAL NOUN _____

PLURAL NOUN _____

ADJECTIVE _____

PLURAL NOUN _____

NOUN _____

PLURAL NOUN _____

VERB _____

NUMBER _____

NOUN _____

NUMBER _____

ADVERB _____

NOUN _____

PLURAL NOUN _____

VERB _____

# MAD LIBS®
# GOING CAROLING

'Tis the _____ season for caroling! Here's how to make
                ADJECTIVE

everyone's Christmas a little more merry and _____:
                                                    ADJECTIVE

• Gather _____ of your _____ friends and family
              NUMBER                      ADJECTIVE

_____ together. Pick out a few classic _____
   PLURAL NOUN                                              PLURAL NOUN

to sing, like "Have Yourself a/an _____ Little Christmas," "Silver
                                        ADJECTIVE

_____," and "Frosty the _____-man."
   PLURAL NOUN                              NOUN

• Put Santa _____ on everyone's heads and _____
                 PLURAL NOUN                                      VERB

to your neighbor's house.

• Knock _____ times on the front _____. Nothing?
             NUMBER                                  NOUN

Knock _____ more times _____.
           NUMBER                          ADVERB

• When your neighbor answers the _____, ask if he or she
                                       NOUN

would like to hear you sing a song. If your neighbor says yes, sing your

_____ out. If your neighbor says no, _____
   PLURAL NOUN                                            VERB

anyway!

MAD LIBS® is fun to play with friends, but you can also play it by yourself! To begin with, DO NOT look at the story on the page below. Fill in the blanks on this page with the words called for. Then, using the words you have selected, fill in the blank spaces in the story.

Now you've created your own hilarious MAD LIBS® game!

## DECK THE HALLS

PLURAL NOUN _____

PLURAL NOUN _____

NOUN _____

ADJECTIVE _____

ADJECTIVE _____

ADJECTIVE _____

VERB ENDING IN "ING" _____

NOUN _____

ADJECTIVE _____

ADJECTIVE _____

# MAD LIBS®
# DECK THE HALLS

Deck the _____ with boughs of _____.
　　　　　PLURAL NOUN　　　　　　　　　　　　PLURAL NOUN

Fa-la-la-la-la-la-la-la-la!

'Tis the _____ to be _____.
　　　　　NOUN　　　　　　　　　　ADJECTIVE

Fa-la-la-la-la-la-la-la-la!

Don we now our _____ apparel.
　　　　　　　　ADJECTIVE

Fa-la-la-la-la-la-la-la-la!

Troll the ancient _____ carol.
　　　　　　　　　ADJECTIVE

Fa-la-la-la-la-la-la-la-la!

See the _____ Yule before us.
　　　　VERB ENDING IN "ING"

Fa-la-la-la-la-la-la-la-la!

Strike the _____ and join the chorus.
　　　　　　NOUN

Fa-la-la-la-la-la-la-la-la!

Follow me in _____ measure.
　　　　　　ADJECTIVE

Fa-la-la-la-la-la-la-la-la!

While I tell of _____ treasure.
　　　　　　　ADJECTIVE

Fa-la-la-la-la-la-la-la-la!

MAD LIBS® is fun to play with friends, but you can also play it by yourself! To begin with, DO NOT look at the story on the page below. Fill in the blanks on this page with the words called for. Then, using the words you have selected, fill in the blank spaces in the story.

Now you've created your own hilarious MAD LIBS® game!

# THE TWELVE DAYS OF CHRISTMAS, PART 1

NOUN _____

ADJECTIVE _____

NOUN _____

ADJECTIVE _____

NOUN _____

ADJECTIVE _____

ADJECTIVE _____

NOUN _____

PLURAL NOUN _____

ADJECTIVE _____

NOUN _____

On the first day of Christmas,

My true _____ gave to me
NOUN

A partridge in a/an _____ tree.
ADJECTIVE

On the second _____ of Christmas,
NOUN

My _____ love gave to me
ADJECTIVE

Two turtledoves

And a/an _____ in a/an _____ tree.
NOUN                           ADJECTIVE

On the third day of Christmas,

My _____ _____ gave to me
ADJECTIVE          NOUN

Three French hens,

Two turtle-_____,
PLURAL NOUN

And a partridge in a/an _____ _____.
ADJECTIVE          NOUN

MAD LIBS® is fun to play with friends, but you can also play it by yourself! To begin with, DO NOT look at the story on the page below. Fill in the blanks on this page with the words called for. Then, using the words you have selected, fill in the blank spaces in the story.

Now you've created your own hilarious MAD LIBS® game!

## THE TWELVE DAYS OF CHRISTMAS, PART 2

NOUN _____

NUMBER _____

ADJECTIVE _____

NOUN _____

ADJECTIVE _____

NOUN _____

PLURAL NOUN _____

PLURAL NOUN _____

ADJECTIVE _____

PLURAL NOUN _____

ADJECTIVE _____

PLURAL NOUN _____

NOUN _____

ADJECTIVE _____

NOUN _____

# MAD LIBS®

# THE TWELVE DAYS OF CHRISTMAS, PART 2

On the fourth day of Christmas,

My true _____ gave to me
                NOUN

Four calling birds,

_____ French hens,
        NUMBER

Two _____-doves,
        ADJECTIVE

And a/an _____ in a pear tree.
                NOUN


On the fifth day of Christmas,

My _____ _____ gave to me
        ADJECTIVE              NOUN

Five golden _____,
                PLURAL NOUN

Four calling _____,
                PLURAL NOUN

Three _____ _____,
        ADJECTIVE            PLURAL NOUN

Two _____ _____,
        ADJECTIVE            PLURAL NOUN

And a/an _____ in a/an _____ _____.
                NOUN                    ADJECTIVE            NOUN

MAD LIBS® is fun to play with friends, but you can also play it by yourself! To begin with, DO NOT look at the story on the page below. Fill in the blanks on this page with the words called for. Then, using the words you have selected, fill in the blank spaces in the story.

Now you've created your own hilarious MAD LIBS® game!

## CHRISTMAS SHOPPING

ADJECTIVE _____

ADJECTIVE _____

PLURAL NOUN _____

NOUN _____

CELEBRITY _____

VERB (PAST TENSE) _____

VERB _____

ADJECTIVE _____

NOUN _____

TYPE OF LIQUID _____

ADJECTIVE _____

ADJECTIVE _____

NOUN _____

PLURAL NOUN _____

PLURAL NOUN _____

NOUN _____

VERB ENDING IN "ING" _____

# MAD LIBS®
# CHRISTMAS SHOPPING

When I was a/an _____ kid, I loved going to the _____
                         ADJECTIVE                                    ADJECTIVE

mall at Christmastime. My parents would dress me and my _____
                                                            PLURAL NOUN

in our cutest holiday outfits. Then we'd all pile into the family _____
                                                                       NOUN

and drive to the mall to sit on _____'s lap. As we _____
                                   CELEBRITY                  VERB (PAST TENSE)

in the long line to Santa's _____-shop, we'd look around at all
                                  VERB

the _____ lights strung around the _____,
         ADJECTIVE                                    NOUN

drink hot _____, and sing _____ carols. Then the
             TYPE OF LIQUID               ADJECTIVE

_____ moment would arrive—we'd finally get to meet Santa
     ADJECTIVE

and tell him what we wanted to find under the _____ on
                                                    NOUN

Christmas morning. Of course, now that I'm older, I avoid the mall at all

_____. These days, I buy all my _____ online.
     PLURAL NOUN                               PLURAL NOUN

With just a click of the _____, Christmas _____
                              NOUN                          VERB ENDING IN "ING"

couldn't be easier!

MAD LIBS® is fun to play with friends, but you can also play it by yourself! To begin with, DO NOT look at the story on the page below. Fill in the blanks on this page with the words called for. Then, using the words you have selected, fill in the blank spaces in the story.

Now you've created your own hilarious MAD LIBS® game!

---

# THE CHRISTMAS PAGEANT

ADJECTIVE _____

A PLACE _____

PLURAL NOUN _____

PLURAL NOUN _____

ADJECTIVE _____

NOUN _____

NOUN _____

SILLY WORD _____

PERSON IN ROOM (MALE) _____

NOUN _____

ADJECTIVE _____

ADJECTIVE _____

COLOR _____

NOUN _____

ADJECTIVE _____

PART OF THE BODY (PLURAL) _____

PLURAL NOUN _____

SILLY WORD _____

# MAD LIBS®
# THE CHRISTMAS PAGEANT

Every December, our school puts on a/an _____ holiday pageant.
ADJECTIVE

We decorate (the) _____ with snow-_____ and red
A PLACE PLURAL NOUN

and green _____, and we perform a/an _____ play
PLURAL NOUN ADJECTIVE

and sing Christmas carols. This year, the _____ is set in the North
NOUN

Pole. Our music _____, Mrs. _____, cast my best
NOUN SILLY WORD

friend, _____, as Santa. He will, of course, be wearing a red
PERSON IN ROOM (MALE)

_____ stuffed with a/an _____ pillow so he'll look
NOUN ADJECTIVE

really _____. I was cast as Rudolph the _____-nosed
ADJECTIVE COLOR

_____. I'll be wearing _____ antlers on my
NOUN ADJECTIVE

_____. The rest of the class will be elves making
PART OF THE BODY (PLURAL)

_____ in Santa's workshop. I can't wait! Ho, _____, ho!
PLURAL NOUN SILLY WORD

MAD LIBS® is fun to play with friends, but you can also play it by yourself! To begin with, DO NOT look at the story on the page below. Fill in the blanks on this page with the words called for. Then, using the words you have selected, fill in the blank spaces in the story.

Now you've created your own hilarious MAD LIBS® game!

## O CHRISTMAS TREE

NOUN _____

SAME NOUN _____

ADJECTIVE _____

NOUN _____

SAME NOUN _____

ADJECTIVE _____

ADJECTIVE _____

PLURAL NOUN _____

ADJECTIVE _____

PLURAL NOUN _____

NOUN _____

SAME NOUN _____

ADJECTIVE _____

# MAD LIBS®
# O CHRISTMAS TREE

O Christmas _____, O Christmas _____,
                    NOUN                              SAME NOUN

How _____ are your branches!
            ADJECTIVE

O Christmas _____, O Christmas _____,
                    NOUN                              SAME NOUN

How _____ are your branches!
            ADJECTIVE

They're _____ when summer _____ are bright.
                ADJECTIVE                         PLURAL NOUN

They're _____ when winter _____ are white.
                ADJECTIVE                         PLURAL NOUN

O Christmas _____, O Christmas _____,
                    NOUN                              SAME NOUN

How _____ are your branches!
            ADJECTIVE

MAD LIBS® is fun to play with friends, but you can also play it by yourself! To begin with, DO NOT look at the story on the page below. Fill in the blanks on this page with the words called for. Then, using the words you have selected, fill in the blank spaces in the story.

Now you've created your own hilarious MAD LIBS® game!

## UP ON THE HOUSETOP

NOUN _____

ANIMAL (PLURAL) _____

ADJECTIVE _____

NOUN _____

ADJECTIVE _____

PERSON IN ROOM _____

PLURAL NOUN _____

EXCLAMATION _____

NOUN _____

VERB _____

PERSON IN ROOM _____

NOUN _____

SILLY WORD _____

SAME SILLY WORD _____

SAME SILLY WORD _____

ADJECTIVE _____

# MAD LIBS®
## UP ON THE HOUSETOP

Up on the _____-top, _____ pause.
    NOUN            ANIMAL (PLURAL)

Out jumps _____, old Santa Claus.
            ADJECTIVE

Down through the _____ with lots of toys,
                    NOUN

All for the _____ ones, Christmas joys.
              ADJECTIVE

Ho, ho, ho! Who wouldn't go? Ho, ho, ho! _____ wouldn't go!
                                            PERSON IN ROOM


First comes the _____ of little Nell.
                  PLURAL NOUN

_____! Dear Santa, fill it well!
  EXCLAMATION

Give her a/an _____ that laughs and cries,
                NOUN

One that will _____ and shut its eyes.
                VERB

Ho, ho, ho! Who wouldn't go? Ho, ho, ho! _____ wouldn't go!
                                            PERSON IN ROOM


Up on the _____-top, _____, _____,
            NOUN              SILLY WORD       SAME SILLY WORD

_____!
SAME SILLY WORD

Down through the chimney with _____ Saint Nick.
                                ADJECTIVE

MAD LIBS® is fun to play with friends, but you can also play it by yourself! To begin with, DO NOT look at the story on the page below. Fill in the blanks on this page with the words called for. Then, using the words you have selected, fill in the blank spaces in the story.

Now you've created your own hilarious MAD LIBS® game!

# A CHRISTMAS SOLO

NOUN _____

ADVERB _____

ADJECTIVE _____

VERB ENDING IN "ING" _____

NUMBER _____

NOUN _____

VERB (PAST TENSE) _____

COLOR _____

PART OF THE BODY _____

PERSON IN ROOM _____

ADJECTIVE _____

PLURAL NOUN _____

ADJECTIVE _____

PLURAL NOUN _____

ADJECTIVE _____

VERB (PAST TENSE) _____

SAME VERB (PAST TENSE) _____

NOUN _____

ADJECTIVE _____

# MAD LIBS®
# A CHRISTMAS SOLO

A few years ago, my music _____ asked me to sing a Christmas
                              NOUN

solo at our holiday concert. At first I was _____ flattered, but the
                                            ADVERB

more I thought about it, the more _____ I became. Every time I
                                  ADJECTIVE

thought about _____ in front of _____ people,
              VERB ENDING IN "ING"            NUMBER

my whole _____ started to shake. What if I _____
         NOUN                                          VERB (PAST TENSE)

or forgot the lyrics? What if I suddenly developed a/an _____
                                                        COLOR

rash on my _____? My friend _____ suggested
           PART OF THE BODY             PERSON IN ROOM

picturing the audience as a bunch of _____ _____
                                     ADJECTIVE          PLURAL NOUN

to make it easier. That seemed like a/an _____ plan—
                                         ADJECTIVE

until I worried I'd start laughing and all the _____ would
                                               PLURAL NOUN

think I was _____. Finally, the night of the concert arrived.
            ADJECTIVE

I walked onstage, gathered all my courage, and _____ like
                                               VERB (PAST TENSE)

I'd never _____ before. The song went off without a/an
          SAME VERB (PAST TENSE)

_____, and I received a standing ovation. It was the most
NOUN

_____ moment of my entire life!
ADJECTIVE

MAD LIBS® is fun to play with friends, but you can also play it by yourself! To begin with, DO NOT look at the story on the page below. Fill in the blanks on this page with the words called for. Then, using the words you have selected, fill in the blank spaces in the story.

Now you've created your own hilarious MAD LIBS® game!

# AUNTIE'S CRAZY CHRISTMAS CLOTHING

PLURAL NOUN _____

PLURAL NOUN _____

ADJECTIVE _____

PERSON IN ROOM (FEMALE) _____

ADJECTIVE _____

PLURAL NOUN _____

PLURAL NOUN _____

PART OF THE BODY _____

PLURAL NOUN _____

COLOR _____

A PLACE _____

NOUN _____

PART OF THE BODY _____

VERB (PAST TENSE) _____

PART OF THE BODY _____

# MAD LIBS®
# AUNTIE'S CRAZY CHRISTMAS CLOTHING

Every Christmas, my family gets together to exchange _____ and
PLURAL NOUN

eat a big Christmas dinner of ham, mashed _____, and all the
PLURAL NOUN

_____ trimmings. For me, though, the highlight of every Christmas
ADJECTIVE

is seeing my aunt _____ make her _____
PERSON IN ROOM (FEMALE)                          ADJECTIVE

entrance. She always wears the craziest _____ on Christmas. You
PLURAL NOUN

wouldn't believe it! For example, last year she wore earrings that looked like

giant Christmas _____, a sweatshirt with Santa's _____
PLURAL NOUN                                         PART OF THE BODY

on the front, and socks with red and white candy _____ on
PLURAL NOUN

them. She also wore a snowflake pin with a flashing _____
COLOR

light that played "Santa Claus Is Coming to (the) _____," and
A PLACE

she carried a/an _____ made out of tinsel. To top it all off,
NOUN

she tied bells to her _____ so she would jingle when she
PART OF THE BODY

_____! Gosh, that was almost as funny as the year she wrapped
VERB (PAST TENSE)

her entire _____ in Christmas lights! I can't wait to see what
PART OF THE BODY

she'll wear this year.

MAD LIBS® is fun to play with friends, but you can also play it by yourself! To begin with, DO NOT look at the story on the page below. Fill in the blanks on this page with the words called for. Then, using the words you have selected, fill in the blank spaces in the story.

Now you've created your own hilarious MAD LIBS® game!

# 'TWAS THE NIGHT BEFORE CHRISTMAS, PART 1

NOUN _____

ANIMAL _____

PLURAL NOUN _____

CELEBRITY (MALE) _____

ADJECTIVE _____

NUMBER _____

ADJECTIVE _____

ADJECTIVE _____

SAME CELEBRITY (MALE) _____

PLURAL NOUN _____

VERB (PAST TENSE) _____

VERB (PAST TENSE) _____

PERSON IN ROOM _____

SILLY WORD _____

SILLY WORD _____

SILLY WORD _____

NOUN _____

VERB _____

VERB _____

VERB _____

# MAD LIBS®
## 'TWAS THE NIGHT BEFORE CHRISTMAS, PART 1

'Twas the night before Christmas, when all through the _____,
NOUN

Not a creature was stirring, not even a/an _____.
ANIMAL

The _____ were hung by the chimney with care,
PLURAL NOUN

In hopes that _____ soon would be there.
CELEBRITY (MALE)

When what to my wondering eyes should appear,

But a/an _____ sleigh and _____
ADJECTIVE                                  NUMBER

_____ reindeer.
ADJECTIVE

With a little old driver, so _____ and quick,
ADJECTIVE

I knew in a moment it must be _____.
SAME CELEBRITY (MALE)

More rapid than _____, his reindeer they came,
PLURAL NOUN

As he _____ and _____ and called them by name:
VERB (PAST TENSE)        VERB (PAST TENSE)

"Now, _____! Now, Dancer! Now, _____
PERSON IN ROOM                              SILLY WORD

and Vixen!

On, _____! On, Cupid! On, _____ and Blitzen!
SILLY WORD                          SILLY WORD

To the top of the _____! To the top of the wall!
NOUN

Now _____ away! _____ away! _____ away, all!"
VERB                    VERB                    VERB

MAD LIBS® is fun to play with friends, but you can also play it by yourself! To begin with, DO NOT look at the story on the page below. Fill in the blanks on this page with the words called for. Then, using the words you have selected, fill in the blank spaces in the story.

Now you've created your own hilarious MAD LIBS® game!

# 'TWAS THE NIGHT BEFORE CHRISTMAS, PART 2

NOUN _____

VERB ENDING IN "ING" _____

VERB ENDING IN "ING" _____

ADJECTIVE _____

CELEBRITY (FROM PART 1) _____

PLURAL NOUN _____

PLURAL NOUN _____

VERB (PAST TENSE) _____

PLURAL NOUN _____

VERB (PAST TENSE) _____

PART OF THE BODY _____

NOUN _____

VERB (PAST TENSE) _____

ADJECTIVE _____

ADJECTIVE _____

# MAD LIBS®
## 'TWAS THE NIGHT BEFORE CHRISTMAS, PART 2

And then, in a twinkling, I heard on the _____
                                          NOUN

The _____ and _____ of each
        VERB ENDING IN "ING"              VERB ENDING IN "ING"

_____ hoof.
   ADJECTIVE

And down the chimney _____ came, amid _____
                      CELEBRITY (FROM PART 1)              PLURAL NOUN

and soot.

He was covered in _____ from his head to his foot.
                     PLURAL NOUN

He _____ not a word, but went straight to his work,
    VERB (PAST TENSE)

And filled all the _____, then _____ with a jerk.
                      PLURAL NOUN              VERB (PAST TENSE)

And laying his _____ aside of his nose,
                 PART OF THE BODY

And giving a nod, up the _____ he rose!
                              NOUN

But I heard him exclaim as he _____ out of sight,
                                VERB (PAST TENSE)

"_____ Christmas to all, and to all a/an _____ night!"
    ADJECTIVE                                              ADJECTIVE

MAD LIBS® is fun to play with friends, but you can also play it by yourself! To begin with, DO NOT look at the story on the page below. Fill in the blanks on this page with the words called for. Then, using the words you have selected, fill in the blank spaces in the story.

Now you've created your own hilarious MAD LIBS® game!

## TOYLAND

NOUN _____

NOUN _____

NOUN _____

VERB _____

ADJECTIVE _____

NOUN _____

ADJECTIVE _____

ADJECTIVE _____

PLURAL NOUN _____

# MAD LIBS®
## TOYLAND

Toyland, _____-land,
        NOUN

Little _____ and _____ land,
        NOUN                  NOUN

While you _____ within it,
          VERB

You are ever _____ there.
             ADJECTIVE


_____'s joy land,
    NOUN

_____, _____ Toyland!
    ADJECTIVE            ADJECTIVE

Once you pass its _____,
                  PLURAL NOUN

You can never return again.

MAD LIBS® is fun to play with friends, but you can also play it by yourself! To begin with, DO NOT look at the story on the page below. Fill in the blanks on this page with the words called for. Then, using the words you have selected, fill in the blank spaces in the story.

Now you've created your own hilarious MAD LIBS® game!

# JOLLY OLD SAINT NICHOLAS

ADJECTIVE _____

PART OF THE BODY _____

NOUN _____

ADJECTIVE _____

NUMBER _____

NOUN _____

ADVERB _____

PLURAL NOUN _____

VERB ENDING IN "ING" _____

ADJECTIVE _____

PLURAL NOUN _____

NOUN _____

ADJECTIVE _____

VERB (PAST TENSE) _____

ADJECTIVE _____

# MAD LIBS®
## JOLLY OLD SAINT NICHOLAS

Jolly _____ Saint Nicholas, lean your _____
     ADJECTIVE                             PART OF THE BODY

this way!

Don't you tell a single _____ what I'm going to say.
                          NOUN

Christmas Eve is coming soon; now you dear _____ man,
                                  ADJECTIVE

Whisper what you'll bring to me; tell me if you can.

When the clock is striking _____, when I'm fast asleep,
                         NUMBER

Down the chimney with your _____, _____ you
                          NOUN              ADVERB

will creep.

All the _____ you will find, _____ in a row;
     PLURAL NOUN                   VERB ENDING IN "ING"

Mine will be the _____ one—you'll be sure to know.
               ADJECTIVE

Johnny wants a pair of _____, Susie wants a/an _____,
                 PLURAL NOUN                NOUN

Nellie wants a/an _____ book—one she hasn't _____.
           ADJECTIVE                    VERB (PAST TENSE)

Now I think I'll leave to you what to give the rest.

Choose for me, _____ Santa Claus. You will know the best.
          ADJECTIVE

MAD LIBS® is fun to play with friends, but you can also play it by yourself! To begin with, DO NOT look at the story on the page below. Fill in the blanks on this page with the words called for. Then, using the words you have selected, fill in the blank spaces in the story.

Now you've created your own hilarious MAD LIBS® game!

# OVER THE RIVER AND THROUGH THE WOOD

CELEBRITY _____

NOUN _____

NOUN _____

ADJECTIVE _____

ADJECTIVE _____

NOUN _____

NOUN _____

VERB _____

PART OF THE BODY (PLURAL) _____

PART OF THE BODY _____

NOUN _____

NOUN _____

NOUN _____

PLURAL NOUN _____

SILLY WORD _____

Over the river and through the wood,

To _____'s house we go.
CELEBRITY

The _____ knows the way to carry the _____
NOUN                                                    NOUN

Though the _____ and _____ snow.
ADJECTIVE                              ADJECTIVE

Over the _____ and through the _____,
NOUN                                          NOUN

Oh, how the wind does _____.
VERB

It stings the _____ and bites the _____,
PART OF THE BODY (PLURAL)              PART OF THE BODY

As over the _____ we go.
NOUN

Over the river and through the _____,
NOUN

To have a full _____ of play.
NOUN

Oh, hear the _____ ringing, "_____-a-ling-ling,"
PLURAL NOUN                          SILLY WORD

For it is Christmas day!

MAD LIBS® is fun to play with friends, but you can also play it by yourself! To begin with, DO NOT look at the story on the page below. Fill in the blanks on this page with the words called for. Then, using the words you have selected, fill in the blank spaces in the story.

Now you've created your own hilarious MAD LIBS® game!

# THE NAUGHTY LIST

ADJECTIVE _____

NOUN _____

ADJECTIVE _____

ADVERB _____

PLURAL NOUN _____

NOUN _____

PLURAL NOUN _____

ADJECTIVE _____

PLURAL NOUN _____

NOUN _____

PART OF THE BODY (PLURAL) _____

NOUN _____

NOUN _____

ADJECTIVE _____

SAME ADJECTIVE _____

# MAD LIBS®
# THE NAUGHTY LIST

Make sure you are always a/an _____ little girl or boy, or you
ADJECTIVE

might get a lump of coal in your _____ at Christmas! Here is a list
NOUN

of _____ things to do and *not* to do to stay off Santa's naughty list:
ADJECTIVE

• ALWAYS play _____ with your brothers and/or sisters, and share
ADVERB

your _____ with them.
PLURAL NOUN

• NEVER make a mess and then blame it on your pet _____.
NOUN

• ALWAYS eat your green _____—even if they taste like
PLURAL NOUN

_____ _____.
ADJECTIVE        PLURAL NOUN

• ALWAYS make your _____ and brush your _____
NOUN                    PART OF THE BODY (PLURAL)

every morning.

• NEVER tell your teacher that your _____ ate your homework
NOUN

unless, of course, you can bring in a well-chewed _____ as proof.
NOUN

• And remember: Santa knows when you've been bad or _____,
ADJECTIVE

so be _____ for goodness' sakes!
SAME ADJECTIVE

MAD LIBS® is fun to play with friends, but you can also play it by yourself! To begin with, DO NOT look at the story on the page below. Fill in the blanks on this page with the words called for. Then, using the words you have selected, fill in the blank spaces in the story.

Now you've created your own hilarious MAD LIBS® game!

## FAVORITE CHRISTMAS CAROLS

ADVERB _____

VERB ENDING IN "ING" _____

ADJECTIVE _____

ADJECTIVE _____

NOUN _____

CELEBRITY _____

COLOR _____

VERB _____

SAME VERB _____

SAME VERB _____

NOUN _____

NOUN _____

NOUN _____

COLOR _____

NOUN _____

# MAD LIBS®
# FAVORITE CHRISTMAS CAROLS

Here's a list of the top ten most _____ played Christmas carols.
                                        ADVERB

Which one is your favorite?

- "The Christmas Song" (also known as "Chestnuts _____
                                                  VERB ENDING IN "ING"

  on a/an _____ Fire")
              ADJECTIVE

- "Have Yourself a Merry _____ Christmas"
                              ADJECTIVE

- "_____ Wonderland"
       NOUN

- "_____ Is Coming to Town"
       CELEBRITY

- "_____ Christmas"
       COLOR

- "Let It _____! Let It _____! Let It _____!"
             VERB                    SAME VERB                 SAME VERB

- "Jingle _____ Rock"
              NOUN

- "Little Drummer _____"
                      NOUN

- "_____ Ride"
       NOUN

- "Rudolph the _____-Nosed _____"
                    COLOR                    NOUN

MAD LIBS® is fun to play with friends, but you can also play it by yourself! To begin with, DO NOT look at the story on the page below. Fill in the blanks on this page with the words called for. Then, using the words you have selected, fill in the blank spaces in the story.

Now you've created your own hilarious MAD LIBS® game!

# WE WISH YOU A MERRY CHRISTMAS

ADJECTIVE _____

SAME ADJECTIVE _____

SAME ADJECTIVE _____

ADJECTIVE _____

ADJECTIVE _____

PLURAL NOUN _____

ADJECTIVE _____

ADJECTIVE _____

ADJECTIVE _____

SAME ADJECTIVE _____

SAME ADJECTIVE _____

NOUN _____

VERB _____

SAME VERB _____

SAME VERB _____

VERB _____

We wish you a/an _____ Christmas,
ADJECTIVE

We wish you a/an _____ Christmas,
SAME ADJECTIVE

We wish you a/an _____ Christmas
SAME ADJECTIVE

And a/an _____ New Year.
ADJECTIVE

_____ tidings we bring
ADJECTIVE

To you and your _____,
PLURAL NOUN

_____ tidings for Christmas
ADJECTIVE

And a/an _____ New Year.
ADJECTIVE

Oh, bring us a/an _____ pudding,
ADJECTIVE

Oh, bring us a/an _____ pudding,
SAME ADJECTIVE

Oh, bring us a/an _____ pudding
SAME ADJECTIVE

And a cup of good _____.
NOUN

We won't _____ until we get some,
VERB

We won't _____ until we get some,
SAME VERB

We won't _____ until we get some,
SAME VERB

So _____ some out here.
VERB

MAD LIBS® is fun to play with friends, but you can also play it by yourself! To begin with, DO NOT look at the story on the page below. Fill in the blanks on this page with the words called for. Then, using the words you have selected, fill in the blank spaces in the story.

Now you've created your own hilarious MAD LIBS® game!

# A CHRISTMAS BLIZZARD!

ADJECTIVE _____

ADJECTIVE _____

PLURAL NOUN _____

ADJECTIVE _____

VERB ENDING IN "ING" _____

ADJECTIVE _____

NOUN _____

NOUN _____

NOUN _____

NOUN _____

NOUN _____

NOUN _____

ADJECTIVE _____

# MAD LIBS®
# A CHRISTMAS BLIZZARD!

Have you been dreaming of a/an _____ Christmas? Me too!
                                  ADJECTIVE

But what do you do when there is a/an _____ blizzard and
                                          ADJECTIVE

you and your _____ get snowed in on Christmas? Here's a/an
                 PLURAL NOUN

_____ list of classic Christmas movies that'll keep everyone
   ADJECTIVE

_____ for hours.
VERB ENDING IN "ING"

    *It's a/an* _____ *Life*
                              ADJECTIVE

    *Miracle on 34th* _____
                                     NOUN

    *A Christmas* _____
                                NOUN

    *How the* _____ *Stole Christmas*
                            NOUN

    *Frosty the Snow-*_____
                                       NOUN

So just grab some pop-_____, throw a few more logs on the
                            NOUN

_____, and keep dreaming of a/an _____ white Christmas!
   NOUN                                           ADJECTIVE

MAD LIBS® is fun to play with friends, but you can also play it by yourself! To begin with, DO NOT look at the story on the page below. Fill in the blanks on this page with the words called for. Then, using the words you have selected, fill in the blank spaces in the story.

Now you've created your own hilarious MAD LIBS® game!

# HERE WE COME A-CAROLING

PLURAL NOUN _____

ADJECTIVE _____

VERB ENDING IN "ING" _____

ADJECTIVE _____

PLURAL NOUN _____

ADJECTIVE _____

ADJECTIVE _____

ADJECTIVE _____

NOUN _____

# MAD LIBS®
# HERE WE COME A-CAROLING

Here we come a-caroling among the _____ so _____.
                                   PLURAL NOUN              ADJECTIVE

Here we come a-_____ so _____ to be seen.
                VERB ENDING IN "ING"      ADJECTIVE

Love and _____ come to you,
          PLURAL NOUN

And to you _____ Christmas, too.
            ADJECTIVE

And we wish you and send you a/an _____ New Year.
                                   ADJECTIVE

And we wish you a/an _____ New _____.
                      ADJECTIVE              NOUN

# MAD LIBS®

## WINTER GAMES MAD LIBS

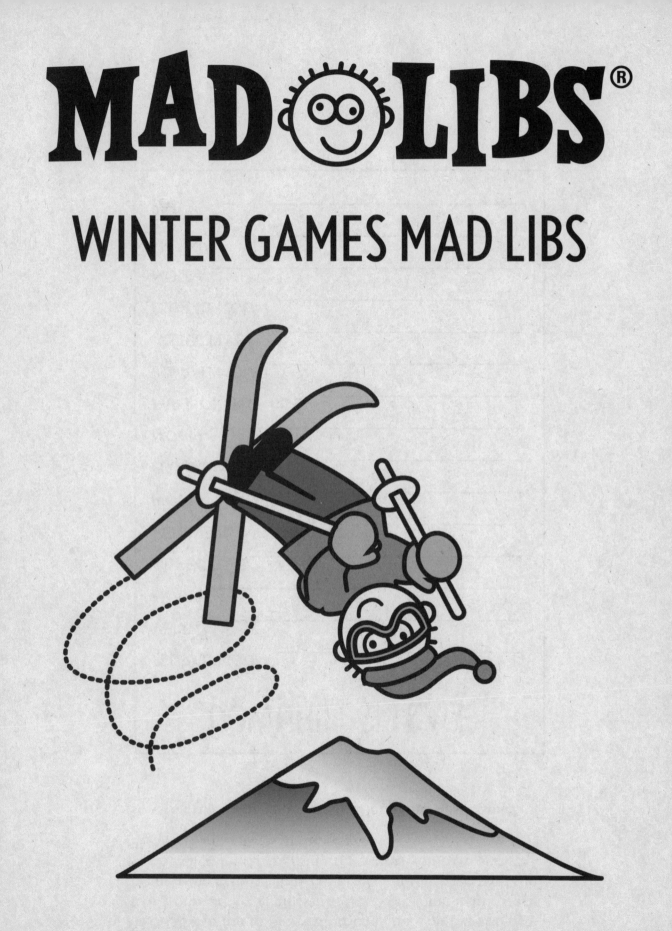

MAD LIBS® is fun to play with friends, but you can also play it by yourself! To begin with, DO NOT look at the story on the page below. Fill in the blanks on this page with the words called for. Then, using the words you have selected, fill in the blank spaces in the story.

Now you've created your own hilarious MAD LIBS® game!

## DOWNHILL SKI RACE

PLURAL NOUN _____

VERB _____

NOUN _____

ADJECTIVE _____

VERB ENDING IN "ING" _____

NOUN _____

PLURAL NOUN _____

NOUN _____

PART OF THE BODY _____

PLURAL NOUN _____

ADJECTIVE _____

PLURAL NOUN _____

NOUN _____

NOUN _____

NOUN _____

# MAD LIBS®
# DOWNHILL SKI RACE

From the moment the downhill _____ leave the gates until
                                                PLURAL NOUN

the second they _____ across the finish line, the ski race is
                            VERB

a/an _____-pounding experience! The skiers must navigate
                NOUN

a/an _____, demanding course: from _____ over
            ADJECTIVE                              VERB ENDING IN "ING"

giant mounds of _____ known as "moguls" to maneuvering
                        NOUN

around plastic _____ planted in the snow to create a more
                    PLURAL NOUN

challenging _____. If that isn't tough enough, the racers
                    NOUN

have to combat the elements—the _____-chilling cold, the
                                        PART OF THE BODY

blinding snow _____, and the _____ winds
                    PLURAL NOUN                    ADJECTIVE

racing up to 100 _____ per hour. Only the results of a
                        PLURAL NOUN

downhill _____ are predictable. It seems that year after year
                NOUN

the same team wins this _____. Must be something in their
                                NOUN

_____!
        NOUN

MAD LIBS® is fun to play with friends, but you can also play it by yourself! To begin with, DO NOT look at the story on the page below. Fill in the blanks on this page with the words called for. Then, using the words you have selected, fill in the blank spaces in the story.

Now you've created your own hilarious MAD LIBS® game!

## TRAITS OF ATHLETES

ADJECTIVE _____

ADJECTIVE _____

NOUN _____

NOUN _____

PLURAL NOUN _____

ADJECTIVE _____

PLURAL NOUN _____

PLURAL NOUN _____

PLURAL NOUN _____

NOUN _____

ADJECTIVE _____

ADJECTIVE _____

PART OF THE BODY _____

# MAD LIBS®
# TRAITS OF ATHLETES

A/An _____ survey of winter-game athletes reveals some very
  ADJECTIVE

_____ statistics:
  ADJECTIVE

• Forty-three percent are ambidextrous. The right _____ always
                                                              NOUN

knows what the left _____ is doing.
                          NOUN

• Ninety-three percent set impossible _____ for themselves and
                                              PLURAL NOUN

then achieve these _____ goals.
                          ADJECTIVE

• Forty-seven percent count their calories and eat well-balanced

_____—observing the recommended allowance of fruits and
  PLURAL NOUN

_____.
  PLURAL NOUN

• Slightly over fifty percent play musical _____, the most popular
                                                    PLURAL NOUN

being the piano, violin, and percussion _____.
                                                NOUN

• Seventy-three percent have a/an _____ sense of timing and
                                          ADJECTIVE

_____ hand-_____ coordination.
  ADJECTIVE              PART OF THE BODY

MAD LIBS® is fun to play with friends, but you can also play it by yourself! To begin with, DO NOT look at the story on the page below. Fill in the blanks on this page with the words called for. Then, using the words you have selected, fill in the blank spaces in the story.

Now you've created your own hilarious MAD LIBS® game!

# FIGURE SKATING

PLURAL NOUN _____

ADJECTIVE _____

NAME OF PERSON (FEMALE) _____

NOUN _____

ADJECTIVE _____

ADJECTIVE _____

ADJECTIVE _____

ADJECTIVE _____

NOUN _____

VERB _____

ADJECTIVE _____

NOUN _____

NOUN _____

NOUN _____

ADJECTIVE _____

NOUN _____

PLURAL NOUN _____

NOUN _____

# MAD LIBS®
# FIGURE SKATING

As a crowd of more than 19,000 _____ filed into the
                                         PLURAL NOUN

_____ auditorium, _____, our
        ADJECTIVE                    NAME OF PERSON (FEMALE)

_____-skating champion, began her _____
        NOUN                                              ADJECTIVE

routine. For the first time in her _____ life, the champion
                                              ADJECTIVE

felt frightened and _____. As the music began, the
                              ADJECTIVE

champion took a/an _____ breath, smoothed the ruffles
                              ADJECTIVE

of her _____, and started to _____. Just as
              NOUN                                VERB

she feared, when it came time for her most _____ jump, a
                                                      ADJECTIVE

triple _____, she lost her balance and landed with a thump
              NOUN

on her _____. She stood up bravely, brushed the ice off her
              NOUN

_____, and finished her _____ routine. The
        NOUN                                    ADJECTIVE

crowd gave her a five-minute standing _____. Even though she
                                              NOUN

realized she had lost the competition, she knew she had won the hearts and

_____ of every _____ in the auditorium.
    PLURAL NOUN                      NOUN

From WINTER GAMES MAD LIBS® • Copyright © 2005 by Penguin Random House LLC.

MAD LIBS® is fun to play with friends, but you can also play it by yourself! To begin with, DO NOT look at the story on the page below. Fill in the blanks on this page with the words called for. Then, using the words you have selected, fill in the blank spaces in the story.

Now you've created your own hilarious MAD LIBS® game!

# RULES FOR A SNOWBALL FIGHT

ADJECTIVE _____

VERB ENDING IN "ING" _____

NOUN _____

PLURAL NOUN _____

PLURAL NOUN _____

NOUN _____

PLURAL NOUN _____

PART OF THE BODY _____

NOUN _____

PLURAL NOUN _____

PLURAL NOUN _____

ADVERB _____

ADJECTIVE _____

NOUN _____

PLURAL NOUN _____

ADJECTIVE _____

PLURAL NOUN _____

PLURAL NOUN _____

The _____ winter games committee does not recognize snowball
    ADJECTIVE

_____ as an official _____. Nevertheless, it has
VERB ENDING IN "ING"    NOUN

established rules and _____ for the athletes who want to throw
    PLURAL NOUN

icy _____ at one another.
 PLURAL NOUN

• Contestants can toss only one _____ at a time and from a
      NOUN

distance not less than twenty-five _____ away.
     PLURAL NOUN

• Aiming at a/an _____ is not permitted. If anybody is hit below
   PART OF THE BODY

the _____, that person automatically wins.
  NOUN

• Loading a snowball with heavy _____ or solid _____
     PLURAL NOUN   PLURAL NOUN

is _____ forbidden. Snowball tampering will result in
  ADVERB

_____ penalties or rejection from the _____.
ADJECTIVE      NOUN

• All _____ must wear _____ gear that protects
 PLURAL NOUN    ADJECTIVE

their eyes, as well as their _____ and _____.
    PLURAL NOUN   PLURAL NOUN

MAD LIBS® is fun to play with friends, but you can also play it by yourself! To begin with, DO NOT look at the story on the page below. Fill in the blanks on this page with the words called for. Then, using the words you have selected, fill in the blank spaces in the story.

Now you've created your own hilarious MAD LIBS® game!

## A WINTER GAME BROADCAST

CELEBRITY (MALE) _____

NOUN _____

NOUN _____

PLURAL NOUN _____

PLURAL NOUN _____

PERSON IN ROOM (MALE) _____

ADJECTIVE _____

NOUN _____

PLURAL NOUN _____

NOUN _____

PLURAL NOUN _____

NOUN _____

ADVERB _____

PLURAL NOUN _____

PLURAL NOUN _____

SAME PERSON IN ROOM (MALE)_____

ADJECTIVE _____

# MAD LIBS®
# A WINTER GAME BROADCAST

Hi, we're broadcasting live from the American compound here at the ski

village. Unfortunately, my cohost, ＿＿＿＿＿＿＿＿＿＿, has laryngitis and
_CELEBRITY (MALE)_

has lost his ＿＿＿＿＿＿＿＿＿＿. He'll be back with us as soon as his
_NOUN_

＿＿＿＿＿＿＿＿＿ returns. Now to breaking ＿＿＿＿＿＿＿＿＿! Sadly, we've
_NOUN_            _PLURAL NOUN_

learned that less than twenty ＿＿＿＿＿＿＿＿ ago, ＿＿＿＿＿＿＿＿＿＿,
_PLURAL NOUN_     _PERSON IN ROOM (MALE)_

America's best ＿＿＿＿＿＿＿＿ skier and favorite to win the giant slalom,
_ADJECTIVE_

suffered a life-threatening ＿＿＿＿＿＿＿＿＿ when he plummeted 300
_NOUN_

＿＿＿＿＿＿＿＿＿ down the side of a/an ＿＿＿＿＿＿＿＿＿. According
_PLURAL NOUN_        _NOUN_

to the latest hospital ＿＿＿＿＿＿＿＿＿, he broke his ＿＿＿＿＿＿＿＿＿,
_PLURAL NOUN_        _NOUN_

but doctors are hopeful he'll heal ＿＿＿＿＿＿＿＿＿ and be back on his
_ADVERB_

＿＿＿＿＿＿＿＿＿ by the end of the year. Our fervent ＿＿＿＿＿＿＿＿ go
_PLURAL NOUN_        _PLURAL NOUN_

out to ＿＿＿＿＿＿＿＿＿＿＿ and his entire ＿＿＿＿＿＿＿＿＿ family.
_SAME PERSON IN ROOM (MALE)_     _ADJECTIVE_

MAD LIBS® is fun to play with friends, but you can also play it by yourself! To begin with, DO NOT look at the story on the page below. Fill in the blanks on this page with the words called for. Then, using the words you have selected, fill in the blank spaces in the story.

Now you've created your own hilarious MAD LIBS® game!

## SNOWBOARDING

PLURAL NOUN _____

NOUN _____

PLURAL NOUN _____

PLURAL NOUN _____

PLURAL NOUN _____

ADJECTIVE _____

ADJECTIVE _____

PLURAL NOUN _____

PART OF THE BODY _____

NOUN _____

PLURAL NOUN _____

VERB _____

NOUN _____

NOUN _____

PLURAL NOUN _____

ADJECTIVE _____

VERB ENDING IN "ING" _____

PLURAL NOUN _____

# MAD LIBS®
# SNOWBOARDING

Most of us have watched snowboarding spring up before our very

_____. In its short history, _____-boarding has
   PLURAL NOUN                   NOUN

cemented itself into the _____ of sporting _____
                    PLURAL NOUN           PLURAL NOUN

around the world. Its simplicity appeals to men and _____
                                      PLURAL NOUN

of all ages. All you need to snowboard are _____ boots, a
                              ADJECTIVE

relatively short _____ board, athletic _____,
             ADJECTIVE              PLURAL NOUN

and a willingness to break a/an _____. I am a high-school
                      PART OF THE BODY

_____ who has won several _____ in
    NOUN                       PLURAL NOUN

snowboarding competitions. Many of my closest friends say I eat, drink, and

_____ snowboarding. I admit to practicing morning, noon, and
   VERB

_____, but it paid off last week when I was invited to qualify for
   NOUN

the team in the freestyle _____. This is where I can shine. I'm the
                  NOUN

best at inverted _____, which are _____, because
          PLURAL NOUN              ADJECTIVE

you're upside down while _____. Excuse me, I'm going now. I
                  VERB ENDING IN "ING"

can't wait to hit the fresh _____ out on the slopes!
                PLURAL NOUN

MAD LIBS® is fun to play with friends, but you can also play it by yourself! To begin with, DO NOT look at the story on the page below. Fill in the blanks on this page with the words called for. Then, using the words you have selected, fill in the blank spaces in the story.

Now you've created your own hilarious MAD LIBS® game!

# BOBSLEDDING GLOSSARY

PLURAL NOUN _____

ADJECTIVE _____

ADJECTIVE _____

NOUN _____

PLURAL NOUN _____

NOUN _____

NOUN _____

NOUN _____

NOUN _____

PLURAL NOUN _____

PLURAL NOUN _____

NOUN _____

VERB ENDING IN "ING" _____

ADJECTIVE _____

VERB _____

NOUN _____

PLURAL NOUN _____

NOUN _____

# MAD LIBS®
# BOBSLEDDING GLOSSARY

The name "bobsledding" comes from the early racers bobbing their

_____ back and forth to gain the most _____
<u>PLURAL NOUN</u> <u>ADJECTIVE</u>

speed. Here are some _____ words and their definitions to
<u>ADJECTIVE</u>

provide a better understanding of this high-speed _____.
<u>NOUN</u>

• **Bobsled:** a large sled made up of two _____ linked together. There
<u>PLURAL NOUN</u>

are two sizes: a two-person _____ and a four-_____ sled.
<u>NOUN</u> <u>NOUN</u>

• **Brakeman:** the last _____ to leap onto the _____.
<u>NOUN</u> <u>NOUN</u>

He/She applies the _____ to bring it to a stop. The brakeman
<u>PLURAL NOUN</u>

must have very strong _____.
<u>PLURAL NOUN</u>

• **Driver:** the front _____ in the bobsled, responsible for
<u>NOUN</u>

_____. The driver's _____ goal is to
<u>VERB ENDING IN "ING"</u> <u>ADJECTIVE</u>

maintain the straightest path down the track.

• **Push Time:** the amount of time required to _____ a/an
<u>VERB</u>

_____ over the first fifty _____ of a run.
<u>NOUN</u> <u>PLURAL NOUN</u>

• **WH:** an abbreviation for "What happened?" Usually said when the

_____ crashes!
<u>NOUN</u>

MAD LIBS® is fun to play with friends, but you can also play it by yourself! To begin with, DO NOT look at the story on the page below. Fill in the blanks on this page with the words called for. Then, using the words you have selected, fill in the blank spaces in the story.

Now you've created your own hilarious MAD LIBS® game!

# SNOWMAN-BUILDING

ADJECTIVE _____

NOUN _____

NOUN _____

ADJECTIVE _____

NOUN _____

ADJECTIVE _____

PLURAL NOUN _____

PART OF THE BODY (PLURAL) _____

NOUN _____

COLOR _____

NOUN _____

PLURAL NOUN _____

ADJECTIVE _____

NOUN _____

NOUN _____

ADJECTIVE _____

NOUN _____

NOUN _____

# MAD LIBS®
# SNOWMAN-BUILDING

Question: What kid hasn't loved the _____ thrill of building a/an
ADJECTIVE

_____-man?
NOUN

Answer: Kids who live where the _____ never stops shining.
NOUN

Nevertheless, snowman-building is one of the most _____
ADJECTIVE

competitions at the winter games. Each team is given several hundred pounds

of powdered _____ to mold and shape into what they hope will be
NOUN

the most _____ snowman anyone has ever laid _____
ADJECTIVE                                                      PLURAL NOUN

on. This year's winner was so adorable that everyone wanted to throw their

_____ around him and hug his _____.
PART OF THE BODY (PLURAL)                                NOUN

They used a bright _____ _____ for his nose,
COLOR                        NOUN

two shiny _____ for his eyes, and a/an _____
PLURAL NOUN                                          ADJECTIVE

_____ on his head for a hat. In addition, they put a corncob
NOUN

_____ in his mouth and tied a/an _____ scarf
NOUN                                           ADJECTIVE

around his neck. Their prizewinning _____ quickly became the
NOUN

talk of the _____.
NOUN

MAD LIBS® is fun to play with friends, but you can also play it by yourself! To begin with, DO NOT look at the story on the page below. Fill in the blanks on this page with the words called for. Then, using the words you have selected, fill in the blank spaces in the story.

Now you've created your own hilarious MAD LIBS® game!

## FACE-OFF

NOUN _____

NOUN _____

ADJECTIVE _____

NOUN _____

NOUN _____

NOUN _____

ADJECTIVE _____

NOUN _____

ADJECTIVE _____

NOUN _____

NOUN _____

PLURAL NOUN _____

ADVERB _____

PLURAL NOUN _____

PLURAL NOUN _____

ADJECTIVE _____

NOUN _____

PLURAL NOUN _____

# MAD LIBS®
# FACE-OFF

If you're seeking fame and _____ as a hockey player, you may
                            NOUN

want to give it a second _____. Hockey is not a sport for the
                          NOUN

_____ of heart! You put your _____ in danger the
ADJECTIVE                                    NOUN

moment you enter the rink and skate onto the _____. Hockey is a
                                              NOUN

game of vicious _____ contact. To be a/an _____
                 NOUN                                    ADJECTIVE

hockey player, you have to keep your _____ in perfect shape,
                                      NOUN

you have to be lean and _____, and you can't afford one
                         ADJECTIVE

extra ounce of _____ on your _____. Hockey
                NOUN                         NOUN

attracts the most volatile _____. These fans can become
                            PLURAL NOUN

_____ physical and throw soda _____, large sticks
ADVERB                                        PLURAL NOUN

and _____, and even _____ coins onto the ice.
     PLURAL NOUN                    ADJECTIVE

You can see why hockey is considered the most physical _____
                                                        NOUN

of all the _____ at the winter games.
            PLURAL NOUN

From WINTER GAMES MAD LIBS® • Copyright © 2005 by Penguin Random House LLC.

MAD LIBS® is fun to play with friends, but you can also play it by yourself! To begin with, DO NOT look at the story on the page below. Fill in the blanks on this page with the words called for. Then, using the words you have selected, fill in the blank spaces in the story.

Now you've created your own hilarious MAD LIBS® game!

## DOGS AND SLEDS

PLURAL NOUN _____

PLURAL NOUN _____

NOUN _____

PART OF THE BODY _____

NOUN _____

NOUN _____

PLURAL NOUN _____

PLURAL NOUN _____

NUMBER _____

ADJECTIVE _____

PLURAL NOUN _____

NOUN _____

NOUN _____

PLURAL NOUN _____

NOUN _____

NOUN _____

# MAD LIBS®
# DOGS AND SLEDS

Of all the winter _____, dogsled racing is my favorite. Watching
              PLURAL NOUN

these beautiful four-legged _____ courageously pull the sled
                        PLURAL NOUN

across the frozen _____ tugs at my _____-strings.
             NOUN                 PART OF THE BODY

The rules for dogsled racing are simple—the first team to cross the finish

_____ wins the _____. A dogsled team consists
    NOUN                  NOUN

of fourteen Siberian _____, each weighing approximately fifty
                   PLURAL NOUN

_____, and each able to pull _____ times its
    PLURAL NOUN                  NUMBER

weight. These beautiful and _____ dogs are trained to respond
                   ADJECTIVE

to the shouted _____ of the _____. The
         PLURAL NOUN             NOUN

driver stands on a/an _____ at the rear of the sled and guides
               NOUN

the dogs with verbal _____ and, if necessary, a crack of the
              PLURAL NOUN

_____. Dogsled races are proof positive why a dog is considered
    NOUN

man's best _____.
           NOUN

MAD LIBS® is fun to play with friends, but you can also play it by yourself! To begin with, DO NOT look at the story on the page below. Fill in the blanks on this page with the words called for. Then, using the words you have selected, fill in the blank spaces in the story.

Now you've created your own hilarious MAD LIBS® game!

## THE LODGE

NOUN _____

NOUN _____

NOUN _____

NOUN _____

PLURAL NOUN _____

NOUN _____

ADJECTIVE _____

NOUN _____

NOUN _____

VERB ENDING IN "ING" _____

PART OF THE BODY _____

NOUN _____

NOUN _____

PLURAL NOUN _____

PLURAL NOUN _____

NOUN _____

ADJECTIVE _____

PLURAL NOUN _____

# MAD LIBS®
## THE LODGE

A/An _____ away from home is most important to a competitive
NOUN

_____. Athletes should select a lodge recommended by a travel
NOUN

_____, the automobile _____, or even relatives and close
NOUN                                    NOUN

_____. The bedroom should have a king-size _____ with
PLURAL NOUN                                                    NOUN

a/an _____ mattress to ensure a good night's _____.
ADJECTIVE                                              NOUN

If possible, there should be a hot _____ to relax those aching
NOUN

muscles after a long day of _____. Since relaxation is so
VERB ENDING IN "ING"

important to an athlete's _____, the lodge should also provide
PART OF THE BODY

an indoor swimming _____. Other amenities might include
NOUN

a wood-burning _____, a game room stocked with arcade
NOUN

_____, game tables for chess or _____, as well
PLURAL NOUN                                  PLURAL NOUN

as a ping-pong _____. Since nutrition is of _____
NOUN                                                  ADJECTIVE

significance to athletes, the lodge's restaurant should have a rating of five

_____.
PLURAL NOUN

MAD LIBS® is fun to play with friends, but you can also play it by yourself! To begin with, DO NOT look at the story on the page below. Fill in the blanks on this page with the words called for. Then, using the words you have selected, fill in the blank spaces in the story.

Now you've created your own hilarious MAD LIBS® game!

## SAGE ADVICE

PERSON IN ROOM _____

VERB ENDING IN "ING" _____

ADJECTIVE _____

ADJECTIVE _____

PLURAL NOUN _____

ADVERB _____

PLURAL NOUN _____

ADJECTIVE _____

PLURAL NOUN _____

NOUN _____

ADJECTIVE _____

PLURAL NOUN _____

PLURAL NOUN _____

VERB ENDING IN "ING" _____

NOUN _____

# MAD LIBS®
# SAGE ADVICE

According to _____, the pioneer of downhill _____,
    PERSON IN ROOM                                              VERB ENDING IN "ING"

"When you ski, your _____ equipment should be the equal of
                        ADJECTIVE

your _____ ability." Remember this sage advice when purchasing
        ADJECTIVE

your first pair of _____. It is _____ important
                      PLURAL NOUN                ADVERB

to take many _____ into consideration before plunking down
                  PLURAL NOUN

_____ bucks for your _____. Your gender,
    ADJECTIVE                        PLURAL NOUN

your height, and your _____ are all _____
                          NOUN                      ADJECTIVE

factors in selecting a pair of _____ that matches your skills and
                                  PLURAL NOUN

_____. It goes without _____: If you don't have the
    PLURAL NOUN                      VERB ENDING IN "ING"

right skis, you're starting off on the wrong _____.
                                                NOUN

MAD LIBS® is fun to play with friends, but you can also play it by yourself! To begin with, DO NOT look at the story on the page below. Fill in the blanks on this page with the words called for. Then, using the words you have selected, fill in the blank spaces in the story.

Now you've created your own hilarious MAD LIBS® game!

# MORE SAGE ADVICE

NOUN _____

NOUN _____

PLURAL NOUN _____

ADVERB _____

ADJECTIVE _____

PART OF THE BODY (PLURAL) _____

NOUN _____

ADJECTIVE _____

NOUN _____

PART OF THE BODY _____

ADJECTIVE _____

NOUN _____

NOUN _____

ADJECTIVE _____

NOUN _____

NOUN _____

# MAD LIBS®
# MORE SAGE ADVICE

Beware! If your skiing equipment isn't top-of-the-_____, you put
<br>NOUN

your _____ at risk. Here are some important _____ to
<br>NOUN                                                      PLURAL NOUN

remember:

• **Ski Boots:** Give careful thought to this important piece of equipment. Choose

_____. Together with ski bindings, these _____ boots
<br>ADVERB                                                          ADJECTIVE

form the link between your skis and your _____.
<br>PART OF THE BODY (PLURAL)

• **Ski Bindings:** As far as your safety is concerned, _____
<br>NOUN

bindings are the most _____ pieces of _____ in skiing.
<br>ADJECTIVE                                            NOUN

• **Ski Helmets:** Protect your _____ by wearing a/an
<br>PART OF THE BODY

_____ ski _____. Helmets absolutely help you
<br>ADJECTIVE                         NOUN

avoid a serious _____.
<br>NOUN

• **Ski Clothing:** First and foremost, get yourself some _____
<br>                                                           ADJECTIVE

underwear, preferably thermal, to keep your _____ warm. You
<br>NOUN

will also need a ski _____ to protect your head and ears from
<br>NOUN

extremely frigid temperatures.

MAD LIBS® is fun to play with friends, but you can also play it by yourself! To begin with, DO NOT look at the story on the page below. Fill in the blanks on this page with the words called for. Then, using the words you have selected, fill in the blank spaces in the story.

Now you've created your own hilarious MAD LIBS® game!

# SLED RACE

NOUN _____

NOUN _____

NOUN _____

PLURAL NOUN _____

NOUN _____

PLURAL NOUN _____

PLURAL NOUN _____

NOUN _____

ADJECTIVE _____

PLURAL NOUN _____

ADJECTIVE _____

NOUN _____

ADJECTIVE _____

NOUN _____

PLURAL NOUN _____

PART OF THE BODY _____

ADJECTIVE _____

PLURAL NOUN _____

# MAD LIBS®
## SLED RACE

Ever since I was in the fifth _____ in school, I've dreamed of
NOUN

having my own sled. I started delivering the morning _____ on
NOUN

my two-wheeler _____ until I saved enough pennies, nickels,
NOUN

and _____ to buy one. It was the smartest _____
PLURAL NOUN                                        NOUN

I ever made. Today, I am a champion sled racer with nine first-place

_____, seven second-place _____, one third-place
PLURAL NOUN                          PLURAL NOUN

_____, and four _____ ribbons. Although some of my
NOUN                       ADJECTIVE

competitors use sophisticated and aerodynamic _____, I still rely
PLURAL NOUN

on a/an _____ version of my old sledding _____.
ADJECTIVE                                            NOUN

Sled racing is relatively simple: The participants line up at the top of a/an

_____ hill. When the starter drops his _____,
ADJECTIVE                                           NOUN

the competitors climb on their _____ and race at break-
PLURAL NOUN

_____ speed to cross the _____ line ahead of the
PART OF THE BODY                     ADJECTIVE

other _____.
PLURAL NOUN

From WINTER GAMES MAD LIBS® • Copyright © 2005 by Penguin Random House LLC.

MAD LIBS® is fun to play with friends, but you can also play it by yourself! To begin with, DO NOT look at the story on the page below. Fill in the blanks on this page with the words called for. Then, using the words you have selected, fill in the blank spaces in the story.

Now you've created your own hilarious MAD LIBS® game!

## SKI JUMPING

NOUN _____

NOUN _____

ADJECTIVE _____

NOUN _____

PLURAL NOUN _____

NOUN _____

ADVERB _____

NOUN _____

ADJECTIVE _____

NOUN _____

NOUN _____

PLURAL NOUN _____

PART OF THE BODY _____

NOUN _____

PART OF THE BODY _____

VERB ENDING IN "ING" _____

PLURAL NOUN _____

PLURAL NOUN _____

# MAD LIBS®
## SKI JUMPING

Whether you're a/an _____ seated in the stands or a/an
                           NOUN

_____ watching on television, the _____ beauty
         NOUN                                              ADJECTIVE

of ski jumping is dramatically apparent. What compares to a skier taking flight,

soaring into the crystal clear _____ against a background of blue
                                         NOUN

_____ with _____-capped mountains looming
    PLURAL NOUN                    NOUN

_____ in the distance? But _____ jumping doesn't
        ADVERB                                          NOUN

shortchange you on thrills. There's _____ drama in every jump.
                                              ADJECTIVE

You can't help but sit on the edge of your _____ and hold your
                                                       NOUN

_____ as conflicting _____ race through your
        NOUN                                PLURAL NOUN

_____. Will the skier break the world _____?
  PART OF THE BODY                                              NOUN

Will he or she break a/an _____? Minutes later, the crowd is
                                PART OF THE BODY

_____ at the top of their _____ and you have
  VERB ENDING IN "ING"                        PLURAL NOUN

your answer: You've got a world champion on your _____.
                                                          PLURAL NOUN

MAD LIBS® is fun to play with friends, but you can also play it by yourself! To begin with, DO NOT look at the story on the page below. Fill in the blanks on this page with the words called for. Then, using the words you have selected, fill in the blank spaces in the story.

Now you've created your own hilarious MAD LIBS® game!

## SPEED SKATING

NOUN _____

ADVERB _____

NOUN _____

PLURAL NOUN _____

PART OF THE BODY (PLURAL) _____

NOUN _____

VERB ENDING IN "ING" _____

NOUN _____

NOUN _____

PLURAL NOUN _____

PLURAL NOUN _____

ADVERB _____

NOUN _____

PART OF THE BODY _____

COLOR _____

# MAD LIBS®
# SPEED SKATING

A speed-skating _____ goes by so _____ that
                        NOUN                              ADVERB

if you blink a/an _____, you might miss the race. In every
                        NOUN

competition, skaters not only race against their fellow _____,
                                                              PLURAL NOUN

they also challenge the _____ of the clock. They know a
                           PART OF THE BODY (PLURAL)

fraction of a/an _____ can be the difference between not only
                        NOUN

winning, but _____ a record. Consequently, skaters worship
                 VERB ENDING IN "ING"

at the shrine of speed. When racing, they skate bent over, angled toward the

ice with one _____ behind them, pressed firmly against their
                    NOUN

_____ to eliminate being slowed down by wind resistance.
     NOUN

They even wear skintight _____ to improve their speed. And,
                              PLURAL NOUN

as you can tell from their trim, muscular _____, skaters are
                                               PLURAL NOUN

_____ weight-conscious. An extra ounce of _____
     ADVERB                                                    NOUN

strikes terror in a skater's _____. To say speed skaters are neurotic
                              PART OF THE BODY

is like calling a kettle _____!
                              COLOR

From WINTER GAMES MAD LIBS® • Copyright © 2005 by Penguin Random House LLC.

MAD LIBS® is fun to play with friends, but you can also play it by yourself! To begin with, DO NOT look at the story on the page below. Fill in the blanks on this page with the words called for. Then, using the words you have selected, fill in the blank spaces in the story.

Now you've created your own hilarious MAD LIBS® game!

# THE LUGE

ADJECTIVE _____

PLURAL NOUN _____

PLURAL NOUN _____

NOUN _____

NOUN _____

PLURAL NOUN _____

PLURAL NOUN _____

NOUN _____

PART OF THE BODY (PLURAL) _____

NOUN _____

NOUN _____

NOUN _____

PART OF THE BODY (PLURAL) _____

ADJECTIVE _____

PLURAL NOUN _____

ADJECTIVE _____

NOUN _____

# MAD LIBS®
# THE LUGE

Although the _____ luge is thought to be relatively new,
           ADJECTIVE

it's actually one of the oldest of all the winter _____. It was
           PLURAL NOUN

a favorite activity of kings, queens, and _____ in the
           PLURAL NOUN

eighteenth century. The word comes from the French _____
           NOUN

for sled. The luge travels at a/an _____-threatening speed,
           NOUN

often exceeding seventy-five _____ per hour. Luge athletes become
           PLURAL NOUN

virtual flying _____ from the moment they step into the
           PLURAL NOUN

_____, lie flat on their _____, and push off
    NOUN           PART OF THE BODY (PLURAL)

with their _____ looking up into the sky. As they fly down the
           NOUN

ice-covered _____, they steer the _____ by
           NOUN           NOUN

pressing their _____ against the front runners. Protected
           PART OF THE BODY (PLURAL)

only by a/an _____ helmet, they risk their _____
           ADJECTIVE           PLURAL NOUN

and are in _____ danger until they speed across the finish
           ADJECTIVE

_____!
    NOUN

MAD LIBS® is fun to play with friends, but you can also play it by yourself! To begin with, DO NOT look at the story on the page below. Fill in the blanks on this page with the words called for. Then, using the words you have selected, fill in the blank spaces in the story.

Now you've created your own hilarious MAD LIBS® game!

# IGLOO-BUILDING CONTEST

ADJECTIVE _____

NOUN _____

PLURAL NOUN _____

ADJECTIVE _____

PLURAL NOUN _____

PLURAL NOUN _____

PLURAL NOUN _____

ADVERB _____

ADJECTIVE _____

PLURAL NOUN _____

NOUN _____

ADVERB _____

NOUN _____

ADJECTIVE _____

ADJECTIVE _____

PLURAL NOUN _____

NOUN _____

ADJECTIVE _____

# MAD LIBS®
# IGLOO-BUILDING CONTEST

Building an igloo is _____ and fun. Good packing snow is
                        ADJECTIVE

required to build a/an _____ with a dome. The first rule is to
                              NOUN

pack the frozen _____ into _____ blocks of all
                    PLURAL NOUN              ADJECTIVE

shapes and _____. Large _____ are used as the
                PLURAL NOUN              PLURAL NOUN

base of the dome and the smaller _____ go on the top. Then,
                                     PLURAL NOUN

each block should be smoothed and angled _____ to make
                                              ADVERB

a/an _____ bond with the other _____. Admittedly,
         ADJECTIVE                          PLURAL NOUN

building a/an _____ is _____ more difficult than
                  NOUN                ADVERB

pitching a/an _____, but it keeps the _____ air
                  NOUN                              ADJECTIVE

out better than a tent. A well-built, average-size igloo can accommodate three

adults or five _____ _____. Believe it or not,
                   ADJECTIVE         PLURAL NOUN

_____-building contests are now being held all over—whenever
    NOUN

the climate is _____.
                   ADJECTIVE

MAD LIBS® is fun to play with friends, but you can also play it by yourself! To begin with, DO NOT look at the story on the page below. Fill in the blanks on this page with the words called for. Then, using the words you have selected, fill in the blank spaces in the story.

Now you've created your own hilarious MAD LIBS® game!

# SKIING DISCIPLINES

ADJECTIVE _____

NOUN _____

PLURAL NOUN _____

ADJECTIVE _____

VERB ENDING IN "ING" _____

ADJECTIVE _____

PLURAL NOUN _____

PLURAL NOUN _____

ADJECTIVE _____

ADJECTIVE _____

ADJECTIVE _____

PLURAL NOUN _____

# MAD LIBS®
# SKIING DISCIPLINES

There are many different types of skiing and each kind has its own

_____ features offering a different kind of excitement and
ADJECTIVE

_____ for skiers of all _____.
NOUN                                            PLURAL NOUN

• **Alpine Skiing:** This _____ form of skiing is the most general
ADJECTIVE

_____ discipline.
VERB ENDING IN "ING"

• **Telemark Skiing:** This is a/an _____ style of skiing. It uses a
ADJECTIVE

turning technique that is admired by many _____ and mastered
PLURAL NOUN

by few _____.
PLURAL NOUN

• **Freestyle Skiing:** This takes skiing to _____ heights, using skis
ADJECTIVE

in many _____ ways to come up with _____ new
ADJECTIVE                                                        ADJECTIVE

tricks, like jumps and _____.
PLURAL NOUN

MAD LIBS® is fun to play with friends, but you can also play it by yourself! To begin with, DO NOT look at the story on the page below. Fill in the blanks on this page with the words called for. Then, using the words you have selected, fill in the blank spaces in the story.

Now you've created your own hilarious MAD LIBS® game!

# Q & A WITH A CHAMPION ICE-FISHER

NOUN _____

NOUN _____

PLURAL NOUN _____

PLURAL NOUN _____

NUMBER _____

NOUN _____

NOUN _____

PLURAL NOUN _____

NOUN _____

PLURAL NOUN _____

NOUN _____

PLURAL NOUN _____

ADJECTIVE _____

NOUN _____

ADJECTIVE _____

# MAD LIBS®
# Q & A WITH A CHAMPION ICE-FISHER

Q: How does it feel to win a gold _____?
                                          NOUN

A: I'm bursting with _____. It's as if I've won a million _____.
                          NOUN                                              PLURAL NOUN

Q: How do you always know there are _____ under the ice?
                                              PLURAL NOUN

A: You don't. You may have to drill more than _____ holes in the
                                                          NUMBER

_____ to catch your first _____.
        NOUN                                      NOUN

Q: When you ice-fish, you're battling the _____. How do you
                                                  PLURAL NOUN

protect yourself against the _____-chilling cold?
                                      NOUN

A: You have to wear protective _____ or you'll freeze your
                                        PLURAL NOUN

_____ off. I suggest heavy boots, wool-lined _____,
        NOUN                                                          PLURAL NOUN

and, of course, _____-johns are a must.
                        ADJECTIVE

Q: When is it better to stay in the comfort of your _____ than go fishing?
                                                          NOUN

A: As my grandfather used to say: "If the wind is from the east, fishing is the

least." I've always followed his _____ advice.
                                          ADJECTIVE

MAD LIBS® is fun to play with friends, but you can also play it by yourself! To begin with, DO NOT look at the story on the page below. Fill in the blanks on this page with the words called for. Then, using the words you have selected, fill in the blank spaces in the story.

Now you've created your own hilarious MAD LIBS® game!

## AWARD CEREMONIES

ADJECTIVE _____

NOUN _____

PLURAL NOUN _____

PLURAL NOUN _____

NOUN _____

PART OF THE BODY _____

ADJECTIVE _____

NOUN _____

ADJECTIVE _____

PLURAL NOUN _____

ADJECTIVE _____

ADJECTIVE _____

PLURAL NOUN _____

PLURAL NOUN _____

# MAD LIBS®
# AWARD CEREMONIES

By far, the most touching and _____ memories of the games are
ADJECTIVE

the _____ ceremonies in which first-, second-, and third-place
NOUN

_____ are presented to the winning _____.
PLURAL NOUN                                        PLURAL NOUN

There's hardly a dry _____ in the stadium when the officials
NOUN

shake the athlete's _____ and place the _____
PART OF THE BODY                              ADJECTIVE

medal around his/her _____. Perhaps the most memorable and
NOUN

meaningful moment occurs when the _____ winner is handed
ADJECTIVE

a bouquet of _____ and the _____ anthem of
PLURAL NOUN                              ADJECTIVE

his/her country is played. When the song ends, the athletes usually break into

_____ smiles, lift their _____ high in the air, and
ADJECTIVE                              PLURAL NOUN

acknowledge the crowd by waving their _____.
PLURAL NOUN

# MAD LIBS®

## CHRISTMAS FUN MAD LIBS

MAD LIBS® is fun to play with friends, but you can also play it by yourself! To begin with, DO NOT look at the story on the page below. Fill in the blanks on this page with the words called for. Then, using the words you have selected, fill in the blank spaces in the story.

Now you've created your own hilarious MAD LIBS® game!

# SELECTING A TREE

ADJECTIVE _____

ADJECTIVE _____

NOUN _____

PLURAL NOUN _____

PLURAL NOUN _____

PLURAL NOUN _____

PLURAL NOUN _____

NOUN _____

ADJECTIVE _____

NOUN _____

PLURAL NOUN _____

PLURAL NOUN _____

ADJECTIVE _____

NOUN _____

ADJECTIVE _____

PLURAL NOUN _____

# MAD LIBS®
# SELECTING A TREE

No Christmas season can be really _____ unless you have
ADJECTIVE

a/an _____ tree in your _____. If you live in
ADJECTIVE          NOUN

a city, you will see many vacant _____ filled with hundreds
PLURAL NOUN

of Christmas _____ for sale, ranging in price from a modest
PLURAL NOUN

few _____ to what many would consider astronomical
PLURAL NOUN

_____. If you live in the country, you can take a sharp
PLURAL NOUN

_____, go to a tree farm or into the _____ forest,
NOUN                                          ADJECTIVE

and chop down your own _____. To make sure your tree is
NOUN

healthy, look for green _____ and shake the tree to make sure
PLURAL NOUN

that _____ don't fall off. Just follow these _____
PLURAL NOUN                                          ADJECTIVE

directions and you will have a perfectly beautiful _____ in your
NOUN

_____ house for _____ to come.
ADJECTIVE                   PLURAL NOUN

Adapted from CHRISTMAS FUN MAD LIBS® • From HOLLY, JOLLY MAD LIBS® • Copyright ©
2009, 2001, 1985 by Penguin Random House LLC.

MAD LIBS® is fun to play with friends, but you can also play it by yourself! To begin with, DO NOT look at the story on the page below. Fill in the blanks on this page with the words called for. Then, using the words you have selected, fill in the blank spaces in the story.

Now you've created your own hilarious MAD LIBS® game!

# DECORATING THE TREE

PLURAL NOUN _____

PERSON IN ROOM _____

ADJECTIVE _____

ADJECTIVE _____

PLURAL NOUN _____

PLURAL NOUN _____

ADJECTIVE _____

ADJECTIVE _____

PLURAL NOUN _____

ADJECTIVE _____

NOUN _____

NOUN _____

ADJECTIVE _____

NOUN _____

PLURAL NOUN _____

NOUN _____

NOUN _____

ADJECTIVE _____

# MAD☺LIBS®
# DECORATING THE TREE

Many people decorate their Christmas _____ on Christmas
                                         PLURAL NOUN

Eve. Last year, _____ had a/an _____
                PERSON IN ROOM                ADJECTIVE

party and everyone helped decorate the _____ tree with tinsel,
                                         ADJECTIVE

_____, and, of course, a string of colored _____.
PLURAL NOUN                                            PLURAL NOUN

A few dozen _____ lights make any tree look more _____.
            ADJECTIVE                                        ADJECTIVE

And most stores sell round, sparkly _____ and little _____
                                     PLURAL NOUN                 ADJECTIVE

balls to hang on the branches. But the hardest _____ to pick is
                                                NOUN

the one that goes right on top. Once that _____ is up, you know
                                           NOUN

the _____ season has officially started. Of course, if you can't
    ADJECTIVE

have a tree for Christmas, you can decorate your _____ or hang
                                                 NOUN

_____ on your _____. The important thing is
PLURAL NOUN              NOUN

to celebrate the _____ so that everyone ends up feeling really
                 NOUN

_____!
ADJECTIVE

Adapted from CHRISTMAS FUN MAD LIBS® • From HOLLY, JOLLY MAD LIBS® • Copyright ©
2009, 2001, 1985 by Penguin Random House LLC.

MAD LIBS® is fun to play with friends, but you can also play it by yourself! To begin with, DO NOT look at the story on the page below. Fill in the blanks on this page with the words called for. Then, using the words you have selected, fill in the blank spaces in the story.

Now you've created your own hilarious MAD LIBS® game!

## WHAT TO GET PEOPLE FOR CHRISTMAS

ADJECTIVE _____

ADJECTIVE _____

PLURAL NOUN _____

ADJECTIVE _____

NOUN _____

PLURAL NOUN _____

NOUN _____

PLURAL NOUN _____

PLURAL NOUN _____

PLURAL NOUN _____

ADJECTIVE _____

NOUN _____

ADJECTIVE _____

ADJECTIVE _____

PART OF THE BODY _____

NOUN _____

NOUN _____

NOUN _____

# MAD LIBS®
# WHAT TO GET PEOPLE FOR CHRISTMAS

One of the _____ things about Christmas is being able to
　　　　　　　ADJECTIVE

pick out _____ presents to give to your relatives and close
　　　　　　　ADJECTIVE

_____. Here are some _____ gift ideas: Don't be too
PLURAL NOUN　　　　　　　　　　　ADJECTIVE

practical. Mom may need a new electric _____ to dice her
　　　　　　　　　　　　　　　　　　　NOUN

vegetables or chop her _____, but think outside the _____
　　　　　　　　　PLURAL NOUN　　　　　　　　　　　　　　NOUN

and buy her something glamorous that she wouldn't buy for herself! Dads are

much easier to buy _____ for. They can always use a new set of
　　　　　　　　　PLURAL NOUN

_____ or, at the very least, a dozen golf _____.
PLURAL NOUN　　　　　　　　　　　　　　　　　　　　　　　PLURAL NOUN

For brothers and sisters, _____ research tells you what's hot.
　　　　　　　　　　　　　ADJECTIVE

A video _____ is an _____ favorite for a/an
　　　　　NOUN　　　　　　　　　ADJECTIVE

_____ brother, and you can win the _____ of a
ADJECTIVE　　　　　　　　　　　　　　　　　　　PART OF THE BODY

sister if you can afford an i-_____. But no matter what you
　　　　　　　　　　　　　　　NOUN

give, remember it is the _____ behind the gift that counts, not
　　　　　　　　　　　　　NOUN

the amount of _____ you spend.
　　　　　　　　NOUN

Adapted from CHRISTMAS FUN MAD LIBS® • From HOLLY, JOLLY MAD LIBS® • Copyright ©
2009, 2001, 1985 by Penguin Random House LLC.

MAD LIBS® is fun to play with friends, but you can also play it by yourself! To begin with, DO NOT look at the story on the page below. Fill in the blanks on this page with the words called for. Then, using the words you have selected, fill in the blank spaces in the story.

Now you've created your own hilarious MAD LIBS® game!

# HOW TO WRAP A PRESENT

PLURAL NOUN _____

ADJECTIVE _____

PLURAL NOUN _____

ADJECTIVE _____

PLURAL NOUN _____

VERB _____

NOUN _____

ADJECTIVE _____

PLURAL NOUN _____

NOUN _____

NOUN _____

ADJECTIVE _____

NOUN _____

ADJECTIVE _____

NOUN _____

ADJECTIVE _____

ADJECTIVE _____

NOUN _____

# MAD LIBS®

# HOW TO WRAP A PRESENT

Before you start to wrap your Christmas _____, make
                                              PLURAL NOUN

sure you have plenty of _____ paper and lots of little gift
                              ADJECTIVE

_____ to place on the packages. Make sure to decorate each gift
  PLURAL NOUN

with _____ bows and _____, and don't forget to
        ADJECTIVE                    PLURAL NOUN

add stickers that say "Do not _____ until Christmas." Place the
                                    VERB

beautifully wrapped _____ under the tree with all the other
                           NOUN

_____ _____. CAUTION: If you are planning
   ADJECTIVE        PLURAL NOUN

to ship a/an _____ out of town, be sure to put it in a sturdy
                   NOUN

_____ and fill every nook and cranny with _____
      NOUN                                               ADJECTIVE

tissue _____ or newspaper. Take this _____
            NOUN                                    ADJECTIVE

package to your local post _____ or schedule a pickup
                                 NOUN

with your _____ carrier. Above all, make sure you get your
              ADJECTIVE

_____ gifts shipped early enough for them to arrive in time for a
   ADJECTIVE

merry _____ for all.
            NOUN

Adapted from CHRISTMAS FUN MAD LIBS® • From HOLLY, JOLLY MAD LIBS® • Copyright ©
2009, 2001, 1985 by Penguin Random House LLC.

MAD LIBS® is fun to play with friends, but you can also play it by yourself! To begin with, DO NOT look at the story on the page below. Fill in the blanks on this page with the words called for. Then, using the words you have selected, fill in the blank spaces in the story.

Now you've created your own hilarious MAD LIBS® game!

## CHRISTMAS DINNER

ADJECTIVE _____

NOUN _____

ADJECTIVE _____

PLURAL NOUN _____

NOUN _____

PART OF THE BODY _____

NOUN _____

ADJECTIVE _____

NUMBER _____

NOUN _____

NOUN _____

NOUN _____

ADJECTIVE _____

NOUN _____

NUMBER _____

ADJECTIVE _____

PART OF THE BODY (PLURAL) _____

PART OF THE BODY (PLURAL) _____

# MAD LIBS®
# CHRISTMAS DINNER

Everyone loves a/an _____ family dinner on Christmas
                        ADJECTIVE

Day. Most families have a huge roasted _____ stuffed with
                                            NOUN

_____ dressing, served with mashed _____ and
   ADJECTIVE                                        PLURAL NOUN

plenty of hot brown _____. If you're cooking your own turkey,
                          NOUN

here is the best _____-licking recipe this side of the Mississippi
                   PART OF THE BODY

_____:
      NOUN

• Rinse the turkey in _____ water and pat it dry.
                          ADJECTIVE

• Brush the turkey with _____ tablespoons of unsalted _____.
                            NUMBER                                      NOUN

• In the cavity of the _____, place one peeled and quartered
                            NOUN

_____ and a/an _____ stalk of celery.
      NOUN                      ADJECTIVE

• Cover the turkey with foil and roast in a preheated _____ for
                                                          NOUN

_____ hours.
   NUMBER

Guarantee: When you serve this turkey, the _____ aroma will
                                                ADJECTIVE

make everyone smack their _____ in anticipation as their
                              PART OF THE BODY (PLURAL)

_____ growl appreciatively.
   PART OF THE BODY (PLURAL)

MAD LIBS® is fun to play with friends, but you can also play it by yourself! To begin with, DO NOT look at the story on the page below. Fill in the blanks on this page with the words called for. Then, using the words you have selected, fill in the blank spaces in the story.

Now you've created your own hilarious MAD LIBS® game!

# TOYS FOR THE KIDS

PLURAL NOUN _____

NOUN _____

PLURAL NOUN _____

VERB (PAST TENSE) _____

PLURAL NOUN _____

NUMBER _____

VERB _____

NOUN _____

ADJECTIVE _____

ADVERB _____

ADVERB _____

ADJECTIVE _____

ADJECTIVE _____

ADJECTIVE _____

NOUN _____

PLURAL NOUN _____

NOUN _____

# MAD LIBS®
# TOYS FOR THE KIDS

Fifty years ago, children received simple _____ such as
PLURAL NOUN

_____-operated _____ or baby dolls that said
NOUN                      PLURAL NOUN

"Mama" when you _____ them. Now kids only want electronic
VERB (PAST TENSE)

_____—even _____-year-olds know how to
PLURAL NOUN              NUMBER

_____ on a computer or text on a cell _____.
VERB                                              NOUN

Today's top-selling toys cater to _____ children's interests, are
ADJECTIVE

_____ sophisticated, and are very _____ priced.
ADVERB                                          ADVERB

But parents beware! By the year 2020, children will expect to have their own

_____ space shuttles and _____ robots to do
ADJECTIVE                             ADJECTIVE

their _____ homework and perform such chores as taking out
ADJECTIVE

the _____, washing the _____, and even walking
NOUN                              PLURAL NOUN

the _____.
NOUN

MAD LIBS® is fun to play with friends, but you can also play it by yourself! To begin with, DO NOT look at the story on the page below. Fill in the blanks on this page with the words called for. Then, using the words you have selected, fill in the blank spaces in the story.

Now you've created your own hilarious MAD LIBS® game!

# A LETTER TO SANTA

PERSON IN ROOM _____

NOUN _____

ADJECTIVE _____

NOUN _____

PART OF THE BODY _____

ADVERB _____

NOUN _____

NUMBER _____

PLURAL NOUN _____

PLURAL NOUN _____

NOUN _____

ADJECTIVE _____

NOUN _____

NOUN _____

NOUN _____

ADJECTIVE _____

ADJECTIVE _____

NOUN _____

# MAD LIBS®
# A LETTER TO SANTA

My name is _____, and all year I have been a very, very good
<small>PERSON IN ROOM</small>

_____, especially at my _____ school. Whenever
<small>NOUN</small> <small>ADJECTIVE</small>

my teacher asked me to clean the _____, I put a smile on my
<small>NOUN</small>

_____ and _____ did it. And this winter, when the
<small>PART OF THE BODY</small> <small>ADVERB</small>

streets were covered with ice and _____, I helped more than
<small>NOUN</small>

_____ old _____ cross the street (and I kept
<small>NUMBER</small> <small>PLURAL NOUN</small>

a record). I hope these are enough good _____ to justify your
<small>PLURAL NOUN</small>

giving me the brand-new _____ with the _____
<small>NOUN</small> <small>ADJECTIVE</small>

wheels I asked for on my Christmas _____. And if you're still
<small>NOUN</small>

in a giving mood, I could also use a new tennis _____ and a
<small>NOUN</small>

high-definition _____. Santa, thank you for taking the time to
<small>NOUN</small>

read this _____ letter. I know, I just know, that I will wake up on
<small>ADJECTIVE</small>

Christmas morning and find everything on my _____ list under
<small>ADJECTIVE</small>

the Christmas _____. If not, I guess I will have been good for nothing.
<small>NOUN</small>

MAD LIBS® is fun to play with friends, but you can also play it by yourself! To begin with, DO NOT look at the story on the page below. Fill in the blanks on this page with the words called for. Then, using the words you have selected, fill in the blank spaces in the story.

Now you've created your own hilarious MAD LIBS® game!

# SANTA'S BIG DAY

ADJECTIVE _____

PLURAL NOUN _____

NOUN _____

ADJECTIVE _____

PLURAL NOUN _____

PLURAL NOUN _____

PLURAL NOUN _____

NOUN _____

ADJECTIVE _____

PLURAL NOUN _____

NOUN _____

NOUN _____

PLURAL NOUN _____

ADJECTIVE _____

NOUN _____

ADJECTIVE _____

PLURAL NOUN _____

ADJECTIVE _____

# MAD LIBS®
## SANTA'S BIG DAY

Santa Claus has a very _____ life. He lives at the North Pole
                              ADJECTIVE

surrounded 24/7 by snow and _____. He works around the
                                   PLURAL NOUN

_____ in his workshop. He has _____ little
        NOUN                                      ADJECTIVE

elves helping him make _____ and _____
                              PLURAL NOUN              PLURAL NOUN

for him to give to children on Christmas. On Christmas Eve, these industrious

_____ load up Santa's _____ with the
        PLURAL NOUN                        NOUN

_____ presents. Then Santa hitches his sled to his team of nine
   ADJECTIVE

_____ and goes flying through the sky. When he sees a child's
   PLURAL NOUN

_____, he lands on the roof, slides down the _____,
        NOUN                                                    NOUN

and spends magical moments filling the _____ the children have
                                           PLURAL NOUN

hung on the mantelpiece and putting _____ gifts under their
                                          ADJECTIVE

Christmas _____. Then it's back up the chimney and into the
               NOUN

_____ blue yonder to make another child's _____
   ADJECTIVE                                              PLURAL NOUN

come true. Santa certainly leads a/an _____ life!
                                          ADJECTIVE

Adapted from CHRISTMAS FUN MAD LIBS® • From HOLLY, JOLLY MAD LIBS® • Copyright ©
2009, 2001, 1985 by Penguin Random House LLC.

MAD LIBS® is fun to play with friends, but you can also play it by yourself! To begin with, DO NOT look at the story on the page below. Fill in the blanks on this page with the words called for. Then, using the words you have selected, fill in the blank spaces in the story.

Now you've created your own hilarious MAD LIBS® game!

# GOING TO SEE SANTA

PERSON IN ROOM _____

NOUN _____

ADJECTIVE _____

VERB _____

ADJECTIVE _____

ADJECTIVE _____

NOUN _____

PART OF THE BODY _____

NOUN _____

PART OF THE BODY (PLURAL) _____

NOUN _____

ADJECTIVE _____

NOUN _____

PART OF THE BODY (PLURAL) _____

ADJECTIVE _____

PLURAL NOUN _____

ADJECTIVE _____

# MAD LIBS®
# GOING TO SEE SANTA

Yesterday my friend _____ and I walked across town to see
PERSON IN ROOM

Santa Claus at our local department _____. But there was a long
NOUN

line of _____ kids waiting to _____ with Santa.
      ADJECTIVE                          VERB

As expected, he was a big, round, and _____ man with
                                 ADJECTIVE

a/an _____ beard who wore a bright red _____.
      ADJECTIVE                             NOUN

Whenever a little kid came up to him, Santa would sit the child on his

_____ and ask, "Have you been a good little _____
PART OF THE BODY                                   NOUN

this year?" Without exception, the kids would nod their _____
                                        PART OF THE BODY (PLURAL)

and say, "Yes." Santa would then ask, "And what do you want for Christmas?"

And the most popular answers were "an electric _____" or
                                        NOUN

"a/an _____ doll" or "a two-wheeler _____."
      ADJECTIVE                                 NOUN

Then Santa would say, "You bet." All the kids responded the same way—their

_____ lit up and a/an _____ smile broke
PART OF THE BODY (PLURAL)                            ADJECTIVE

out on their _____. _____ holidays to all!
           PLURAL NOUN                ADJECTIVE

MAD LIBS® is fun to play with friends, but you can also play it by yourself! To begin with, DO NOT look at the story on the page below. Fill in the blanks on this page with the words called for. Then, using the words you have selected, fill in the blank spaces in the story.

Now you've created your own hilarious MAD LIBS® game!

# CHRISTMAS CAROLS

ADJECTIVE _____

ADJECTIVE _____

PLURAL NOUN _____

PLURAL NOUN _____

NOUN _____

PLURAL NOUN _____

NOUN _____

ADJECTIVE _____

NOUN _____

ADJECTIVE _____

PLURAL NOUN _____

ADJECTIVE _____

ADJECTIVE _____

PLURAL NOUN _____

ADJECTIVE _____

ADJECTIVE _____

PLURAL NOUN _____

# MAD LIBS®
# CHRISTMAS CAROLS

Our _____ choir is planning a/an _____ program of
          ADJECTIVE                                    ADJECTIVE

Christmas carols. We will sing on street corners and collect _____
                                                                  PLURAL NOUN

to feed the poor, hungry _____ of Transylvania. Our opening
                              PLURAL NOUN

_____ will be "Jingle _____," followed by
      NOUN                              PLURAL NOUN

"Rudolph, the Red-Nosed _____" and "I'm Dreaming of a/an
                              NOUN

_____ Christmas," and we'll finish up with "Santa Claus Is
      ADJECTIVE

Coming to _____." If an encore is requested, we are prepared
              NOUN

to sing _____ versions of "Deck the Halls with Boughs of
          ADJECTIVE

_____" and "Walking in a/an _____ Wonderland."
   PLURAL NOUN                              ADJECTIVE

Should all go well, we hope to form a/an _____ group, call
                                              ADJECTIVE

ourselves "The _____," and do _____ concerts in
                  PLURAL NOUN                    ADJECTIVE

_____ venues in major _____ all over the world.
   ADJECTIVE                            PLURAL NOUN

Adapted from CHRISTMAS FUN MAD LIBS® • From HOLLY, JOLLY MAD LIBS® • Copyright ©
2009, 2001, 1985 by Penguin Random House LLC.

MAD LIBS® is fun to play with friends, but you can also play it by yourself! To begin with, DO NOT look at the story on the page below. Fill in the blanks on this page with the words called for. Then, using the words you have selected, fill in the blank spaces in the story.

Now you've created your own hilarious MAD LIBS® game!

# A TRANSYLVANIAN NEW YEAR'S

ADJECTIVE _____

ADJECTIVE _____

ADVERB _____

NOUN _____

PLURAL NOUN _____

PLURAL NOUN _____

PART OF THE BODY (PLURAL) _____

ADJECTIVE _____

PLURAL NOUN _____

NOUN _____

NOUN _____

ADJECTIVE _____

NUMBER _____

PLURAL NOUN _____

ADJECTIVE _____

TYPE OF LIQUID_____

NOUN _____

# MAD LIBS®
# A TRANSYLVANIAN NEW YEAR'S

New Year's Day in Transylvania is considered by its _____ citizens
ADJECTIVE

to be their most _____ holiday of the year. On this day, the city
ADJECTIVE

_____ shuts down to celebrate the festive _____.
ADVERB                                                                 NOUN

The locals, who are called _____, spend most of the day dancing
PLURAL NOUN

on the city's ancient cobblestone _____. Holding their loved
PLURAL NOUN

ones in their _____, they perform traditional and
PART OF THE BODY (PLURAL)

_____ Transylvanian _____. The dancing ends
ADJECTIVE                                    PLURAL NOUN

when the _____ sets and night falls—time for the feasts to
NOUN

begin. Every man, woman, and _____ in Transylvania shares
NOUN

a/an _____ meal consisting of more than _____
ADJECTIVE                                                            NUMBER

courses of specially prepared and delicious _____. As always, the
PLURAL NOUN

best part of the evening is the personal appearance of the _____
ADJECTIVE

Count Dracula. In his customary fashion, the count holds up a glass of

_____ and offers his annual toast: "Here's _____
TYPE OF LIQUID                                                       NOUN

in your eye."

Adapted from CHRISTMAS FUN MAD LIBS® • From HOLLY, JOLLY MAD LIBS® • Copyright ©
2009, 2001, 1985 by Penguin Random House LLC.

MAD LIBS® is fun to play with friends, but you can also play it by yourself! To begin with, DO NOT look at the story on the page below. Fill in the blanks on this page with the words called for. Then, using the words you have selected, fill in the blank spaces in the story.

Now you've created your own hilarious MAD LIBS® game!

# NEW YEAR'S RESOLUTIONS

ADJECTIVE _____

ADJECTIVE _____

PART OF THE BODY (PLURAL) _____

NOUN _____

PART OF THE BODY (PLURAL) _____

NOUN _____

PLURAL NOUN _____

PLURAL NOUN _____

PLURAL NOUN _____

ADJECTIVE _____

NOUN _____

ADJECTIVE _____

NOUN _____

NOUN _____

PLURAL NOUN _____

PLURAL NOUN _____

ADJECTIVE _____

# MAD LIBS®
# NEW YEAR'S RESOLUTIONS

According to a/an _____ survey, here are the top New Year's
                        ADJECTIVE

resolutions for kids:

• I will practice _____ hygiene. This includes brushing my
                        ADJECTIVE

_____ after meals, covering my _____
PART OF THE BODY (PLURAL)                              NOUN

when I sneeze, and washing my _____ after I use the
                              PART OF THE BODY (PLURAL)

_____.
        NOUN

• I will eat healthier _____. I will replace fast _____
                          PLURAL NOUN                              PLURAL NOUN

with green _____ and _____ fruit.
              PLURAL NOUN                  ADJECTIVE

• I will pick up after myself. I will make my _____, put my
                                                      NOUN

_____ clothes in the laundry _____, and
        ADJECTIVE                                      NOUN

remember to hang my wet _____ in the bathroom.
                              NOUN

• I will work on being polite to family and _____. I will not respond
                                              PLURAL NOUN

to any _____ my parents ask with _____ answers.
          PLURAL NOUN                              ADJECTIVE

Adapted from CHRISTMAS FUN MAD LIBS® • From HOLLY, JOLLY MAD LIBS® • Copyright ©
2009, 2001, 1985 by Penguin Random House LLC.

MAD LIBS® is fun to play with friends, but you can also play it by yourself! To begin with, DO NOT look at the story on the page below. Fill in the blanks on this page with the words called for. Then, using the words you have selected, fill in the blank spaces in the story.

Now you've created your own hilarious MAD LIBS® game!

## SCROOGE, PART 1

ADJECTIVE _____

NOUN _____

ADJECTIVE _____

ADJECTIVE _____

PLURAL NOUN _____

ADJECTIVE _____

NOUN _____

ADJECTIVE _____

NOUN _____

ADJECTIVE _____

NOUN _____

ADVERB _____

NOUN _____

NOUN _____

# MAD LIBS®
# SCROOGE, PART 1

Of all the _____ English writers of the eighteenth _____,
ADJECTIVE · NOUN

Charles Dickens was the most proficient at creating _____ and
ADJECTIVE

memorable characters. Who among you doesn't remember Ebenezer Scrooge,

the tight-fisted, _____-hearted man who despised Christmas and
ADJECTIVE

all things that brought happiness to _____, young and old? In the
PLURAL NOUN

book's opening chapters, Scrooge is revealed as having _____
ADJECTIVE

contempt for the people in his employ, including his clerk, and only living

_____, Bob Cratchit. Intent on spending Christmas Eve alone
NOUN

in his _____ home, Scrooge is surprised by the visit of the
ADJECTIVE

_____ of Christmas Past, who reveals to Scrooge that most of
NOUN

the _____ events that negatively affected his character occurred
ADJECTIVE

during Christmas holidays. Scrooge is then visited by the Ghost of Christmas

_____, who shows him how the Cratchit family still manages to
NOUN

live _____ on the meager _____ Scrooge pays his
ADVERB · NOUN

loyal _____.
NOUN

Adapted from CHRISTMAS FUN MAD LIBS® • From HOLLY, JOLLY MAD LIBS® • Copyright ©
2009, 2001, 1985 by Penguin Random House LLC.

MAD LIBS® is fun to play with friends, but you can also play it by yourself! To begin with, DO NOT look at the story on the page below. Fill in the blanks on this page with the words called for. Then, using the words you have selected, fill in the blank spaces in the story.

Now you've created your own hilarious MAD LIBS® game!

## SCROOGE, PART 2

ADJECTIVE _____

ADVERB _____

ADJECTIVE _____

NOUN _____

PART OF THE BODY (PLURAL) _____

ADJECTIVE _____

PART OF THE BODY (PLURAL) _____

ADJECTIVE _____

ADJECTIVE _____

ADJECTIVE _____

NOUN _____

PART OF THE BODY (PLURAL) _____

NOUN _____

The Ghost of Christmas Yet to Come shows Scrooge the final consequences of

his _____ actions. Scrooge painfully and _____
    ADJECTIVE                                                    ADVERB

realizes that his life has been meaningless and that his final legacy will be

nothing more than a/an _____ tombstone in an unkept
                           ADJECTIVE

_____-yard. Remorseful, he drops to his _____
    NOUN                                          PART OF THE BODY (PLURAL)

and pleads for a chance to redeem himself. Given the opportunity to repent, he

transforms into a/an _____ model of generosity and kindness and
                       ADJECTIVE

immediately goes on a shopping spree. With his _____ loaded
                                       PART OF THE BODY (PLURAL)

with _____ gifts and _____ food, he races to the
       ADJECTIVE                      ADJECTIVE

Cratchits' home, arriving in time to celebrate the _____ holiday
                                       ADJECTIVE

with his newfound _____. After a traditional Christmas dinner, Scrooge
                    NOUN

and the Cratchits gather in front of the fireplace and comfortably put their

_____ around one another as they happily and harmoniously
PART OF THE BODY (PLURAL)

sing Christmas songs until the wee hours of the _____.
                                       NOUN

Adapted from CHRISTMAS FUN MAD LIBS® • From HOLLY, JOLLY MAD LIBS® • Copyright ©
2009, 2001, 1985 by Penguin Random House LLC.

MAD LIBS® is fun to play with friends, but you can also play it by yourself! To begin with, DO NOT look at the story on the page below. Fill in the blanks on this page with the words called for. Then, using the words you have selected, fill in the blank spaces in the story.

Now you've created your own hilarious MAD LIBS® game!

# THANK-YOU LETTERS

PERSON IN ROOM (FEMALE) _____

ADJECTIVE _____

NOUN _____

PART OF THE BODY _____

VERB _____

PLURAL NOUN _____

ADJECTIVE _____

PERSON IN ROOM (MALE) _____

NOUN _____

PLURAL NOUN _____

PLURAL NOUN _____

PART OF THE BODY _____

ADJECTIVE _____

PERSON IN ROOM _____

NOUN _____

# MAD LIBS®
# THANK-YOU LETTERS

Dear Auntie _____,
PERSON IN ROOM (FEMALE)

I want to thank you for sending me such a/an _____ gift. I've
ADJECTIVE

never had a/an _____ before. It fits my _____
NOUN                                          PART OF THE BODY

perfectly, and it will keep me warm when I have to _____ to
VERB

school in three feet of _____.
PLURAL NOUN

Your _____ nephew,
ADJECTIVE

_____
PERSON IN ROOM (MALE)


Dear Grandma and Grandpa,

I really like the _____ you sent me. It must have cost a lot of
NOUN

_____. It will certainly help me do my homework and it will
PLURAL NOUN

help me get higher _____ this year. I thank you with all my
PLURAL NOUN

_____ for a very _____ gift.
PART OF THE BODY                     ADJECTIVE

Signed,

_____
PERSON IN ROOM

P.S. Mom says I can come to your _____ for a visit next summer.
NOUN

Adapted from CHRISTMAS FUN MAD LIBS® • From HOLLY, JOLLY MAD LIBS® • Copyright ©
2009, 2001, 1985 by Penguin Random House LLC.

MAD LIBS® is fun to play with friends, but you can also play it by yourself! To begin with, DO NOT look at the story on the page below. Fill in the blanks on this page with the words called for. Then, using the words you have selected, fill in the blank spaces in the story.

Now you've created your own hilarious MAD LIBS® game!

# HOLIDAY TRAVEL

PLURAL NOUN _____

PLURAL NOUN _____

NOUN _____

VERB ENDING IN "ING" _____

ADJECTIVE _____

ADJECTIVE _____

NOUN _____

ADJECTIVE _____

ADJECTIVE _____

NOUN _____

PART OF THE BODY _____

NOUN _____

NOUN _____

ADJECTIVE _____

# MAD LIBS®
## HOLIDAY TRAVEL

More _____ travel home to visit their _____
        PLURAL NOUN                                          PLURAL NOUN

during the holidays than at any other time of the _____. If you
                                                           NOUN

choose to travel by plane, it will mean _____ extra time in the
                                          VERB ENDING IN "ING"

airport, with the possibility of a/an _____ delay for any number
                                          ADJECTIVE

of _____ reasons. It is easier to travel by _____
        ADJECTIVE                                                 NOUN

if you are flying with _____ children, but remember this is
                              ADJECTIVE

the time of the year that _____ airlines expect to make lots
                                 ADJECTIVE

of money and, to accomplish this, passengers are packed into planes like

sardines into a/an _____. No matter what the inconvenience,
                          NOUN

bear in _____ that you will still end up getting to your
          PART OF THE BODY

_____ a lot quicker by bus, car, or _____, and
        NOUN                                              NOUN

you'll certainly have more time to spend with your _____ family.
                                                          ADJECTIVE

MAD LIBS® is fun to play with friends, but you can also play it by yourself! To begin with, DO NOT look at the story on the page below. Fill in the blanks on this page with the words called for. Then, using the words you have selected, fill in the blank spaces in the story.

Now you've created your own hilarious MAD LIBS® game!

# BOWL GAMES

ADJECTIVE _____

ADJECTIVE _____

NOUN _____

NUMBER _____

PLURAL NOUN _____

PLURAL NOUN _____

PLURAL NOUN _____

PLURAL NOUN _____

PLURAL NOUN _____

PLURAL NOUN _____

PLURAL NOUN _____

ADVERB _____

ADJECTIVE _____

PLURAL NOUN _____

ADJECTIVE _____

ADJECTIVE _____

ADJECTIVE _____

# MAD LIBS®
# BOWL GAMES

In recent years, the term "bowl" has become synonymous with every

_____ American football post-season matchup between two
ADJECTIVE

_____ college teams. Over the Christmas and New _____'s
ADJECTIVE                                                        NOUN

holidays, there will be, believe it or not, _____ bowl _____
                                                NUMBER              PLURAL NOUN

on television. In living rooms and _____ across the nation,
                                        PLURAL NOUN

families will come together, sit on couches and _____ in front of
                                                      PLURAL NOUN

their TV _____, and snack on popcorn, _____, soft
            PLURAL NOUN                                      PLURAL NOUN

_____, and ice-cold _____. As they watch these
     PLURAL NOUN                          PLURAL NOUN

_____ fought and exciting, _____ games,
        ADVERB                                   ADJECTIVE

these couch _____ will unfortunately have to suffer through
                PLURAL NOUN

a/an _____ number of _____ commercials. But
        ADJECTIVE                         ADJECTIVE

that's the _____ price you pay for free television.
              ADJECTIVE

Adapted from CHRISTMAS FUN MAD LIBS® • From HOLLY, JOLLY MAD LIBS® • Copyright ©
2009, 2001, 1985 by Penguin Random House LLC.

MAD LIBS® is fun to play with friends, but you can also play it by yourself! To begin with, DO NOT look at the story on the page below. Fill in the blanks on this page with the words called for. Then, using the words you have selected, fill in the blank spaces in the story.

Now you've created your own hilarious MAD LIBS® game!

## CHRISTMAS VACATION

ADJECTIVE _____

ADJECTIVE _____

ADJECTIVE _____

ADJECTIVE _____

ADJECTIVE _____

NOUN _____

NOUN _____

NOUN _____

NOUN _____

ADJECTIVE _____

VERB _____

NOUN _____

PLURAL NOUN _____

NOUN _____

PLURAL NOUN _____

NOUN _____

PART OF THE BODY _____

PLURAL NOUN _____

PLURAL NOUN _____

NOUN _____

# MAD LIBS®
# CHRISTMAS VACATION

This year my _____ family—me, my _____ sister,
ADJECTIVE ADJECTIVE

my _____ brother, and my parents—is planning to spend the
ADJECTIVE

holidays in the _____ mountains in a/an _____
ADJECTIVE ADJECTIVE

cabin built by my grand-_____. The cabin is in the middle
NOUN

of a huge _____ on the edge of a/an _____,
NOUN NOUN

which is always frozen at this time of the _____. If the ice is
NOUN

_____ enough, we will be able to _____ on
ADJECTIVE VERB

it. We will decorate the big pine _____ in front of the cabin
NOUN

with Christmas _____. At night, we will build a fire in the
PLURAL NOUN

_____ and toast _____. It promises to be a
NOUN PLURAL NOUN

great _____. On the other _____, next year I
NOUN PART OF THE BODY

hope we can save up enough _____ to afford a trip to one of
PLURAL NOUN

the Hawaiian _____ and celebrate Christmas on a sunny, sandy
PLURAL NOUN

_____.
NOUN

# MAD LIBS®

## COOL MAD LIBS

MAD LIBS® is fun to play with friends, but you can also play it by yourself! To begin with, DO NOT look at the story on the page below. Fill in the blanks on this page with the words called for. Then, using the words you have selected, fill in the blank spaces in the story.

Now you've created your own hilarious MAD LIBS® game!

# HOW TO DATE THE COOLEST GUY/GIRL IN SCHOOL

PLURAL NOUN _____

ADVERB _____

VERB _____

ARTICLE OF CLOTHING _____

PART OF THE BODY _____

NOUN _____

PLURAL NOUN _____

PART OF THE BODY _____

PLURAL NOUN _____

PART OF THE BODY _____

NOUN _____

NOUN _____

VERB ENDING IN "ING" _____

ADJECTIVE _____

ADJECTIVE _____

VERB _____

# MAD LIBS®

## HOW TO DATE THE COOLEST GUY/GIRL IN SCHOOL

It's simple. Turn the _____. Make him/her want _____
                    PLURAL NOUN                                    ADVERB

to date you. Make sure you're always dressed to _____. Each
                                                  VERB

and every day, wear a/an _____ that you know shows off
                          ARTICLE OF CLOTHING

your _____ and makes your _____ look like
      PART OF THE BODY                    NOUN

a million _____. Even if the two of you make meaningful
           PLURAL NOUN

_____ contact, don't admit it. No hugs or _____.
PART OF THE BODY                                        PLURAL NOUN

Just shake his/her _____ firmly. And remember, when he/she
                    PART OF THE BODY

asks you out, even though a chill may run down your _____
                                                     NOUN

and you can't stop your _____ from _____,
                         NOUN                    VERB ENDING IN "ING"

just play it _____. Take a long pause before answering in a very
              ADJECTIVE

_____ voice, "I'll have to _____ it over."
ADJECTIVE                               VERB

MAD LIBS® is fun to play with friends, but you can also play it by yourself! To begin with, DO NOT look at the story on the page below. Fill in the blanks on this page with the words called for. Then, using the words you have selected, fill in the blank spaces in the story.

Now you've created your own hilarious MAD LIBS® game!

## CELL PHONES

NOUN _____

PART OF THE BODY _____

PLURAL NOUN _____

NOUN _____

PLURAL NOUN _____

PLURAL NOUN _____

PLURAL NOUN _____

PLURAL NOUN _____

VERB ENDING IN "ING" _____

ADVERB _____

PART OF THE BODY (PLURAL) _____

VERB _____

ADJECTIVE _____

NOUN _____

PLURAL NOUN _____

NOUN _____

NOUN _____

# MAD LIBS®
# CELL PHONES

No matter where you are these days, you're bound to run into someone with

a cell _____ attached to his/her _____. Even
           NOUN                                PART OF THE BODY

young _____ have _____ phones. Unfortunately,
          PLURAL NOUN                NOUN

they seem to bring out the worst _____ in people. Most cell
                                        PLURAL NOUN

phone users talk with raised _____ in restaurants, museums,
                                PLURAL NOUN

_____, and even in women's and men's _____.
  PLURAL NOUN                                             PLURAL NOUN

Cell phone users think nothing of talking at the same time they are

_____ their cars. This can be _____ dangerous,
VERB ENDING IN "ING"                                 ADVERB

especially when they take their _____ off the road as they
                              PART OF THE BODY (PLURAL)

_____. Pedestrian phone-talkers are also a/an _____
    VERB                                             ADJECTIVE

hazard. Preoccupied with their conversations, they can easily ignore a red

_____ and step in front of oncoming _____,
    NOUN                                       PLURAL NOUN

causing all kinds of _____ accidents and _____ pileups.
                 NOUN                           NOUN

MAD LIBS® is fun to play with friends, but you can also play it by yourself! To begin with, DO NOT look at the story on the page below. Fill in the blanks on this page with the words called for. Then, using the words you have selected, fill in the blank spaces in the story.

Now you've created your own hilarious MAD LIBS® game!

# SPECIALTY OF THE HOUSE

PERSON IN ROOM _____

VERB ENDING IN "ING" _____

PART OF THE BODY _____

ANIMAL _____

SAME PART OF THE BODY _____

NUMBER _____

PLURAL NOUN _____

NOUN _____

VERB (PAST TENSE) _____

TYPE OF FOOD _____

TYPE OF LIQUID _____

ADJECTIVE _____

COLOR _____

NOUN _____

PLURAL NOUN _____

NUMBER _____

COLOR _____

PLURAL NOUN _____

NOUN _____

# MAD LIBS®
## SPECIALTY OF THE HOUSE

Here is Chef _____'s award-_____
  PERSON IN ROOM                              VERB ENDING IN "ING"

recipe for roast _____ of _____: Choose
                      PART OF THE BODY              ANIMAL

a/an _____ weighing about _____
         SAME PART OF THE BODY                            NUMBER

_____. Remove excess _____. Add five cloves
      PLURAL NOUN                              NOUN

of garlic, peeled and _____. Season with two tablespoons of
                          VERB (PAST TENSE)

chopped _____. Add a tablespoon of _____.
             TYPE OF FOOD                                 TYPE OF LIQUID

Sprinkle with a touch of _____ salt. Add a pinch of ground
                              ADJECTIVE

_____ _____. Cook at 350 _____
      COLOR                    NOUN                              PLURAL NOUN

for _____ minutes. Remove from the oven when the skin is
        NUMBER

_____. Serve with mashed _____ and a/an
      COLOR                                      PLURAL NOUN

_____.
      NOUN

MAD LIBS® is fun to play with friends, but you can also play it by yourself! To begin with, DO NOT look at the story on the page below. Fill in the blanks on this page with the words called for. Then, using the words you have selected, fill in the blank spaces in the story.

Now you've created your own hilarious MAD LIBS® game!

## MUSIC

NOUN _____

NOUN _____

ADJECTIVE _____

ADJECTIVE _____

PART OF THE BODY (PLURAL) _____

ADJECTIVE _____

NOUN _____

NOUN _____

NOUN _____

NOUN _____

ADJECTIVE _____

PLURAL NOUN _____

NOUN _____

"Music is the soul of the _____," said Plato. "Music is music is
NOUN

music," said rap _____ I. B. Cool. These two _____
NOUN                                                                  ADJECTIVE

philosophers were right on! When the beat is right, who among us hasn't felt the

_____ urge to snap his or her _____ or break
ADJECTIVE                                          PART OF THE BODY (PLURAL)

out in a/an _____ _____? There's no denying
ADJECTIVE                      NOUN

that music, whether it's a classical _____ by Beethoven or a
NOUN

contemporary _____ by the _____ Brothers, is a/an
NOUN                              NOUN

_____ influence in our daily _____. Music does
ADJECTIVE                                          PLURAL NOUN

indeed soothe the savage _____.
NOUN

MAD LIBS® is fun to play with friends, but you can also play it by yourself! To begin with, DO NOT look at the story on the page below. Fill in the blanks on this page with the words called for. Then, using the words you have selected, fill in the blank spaces in the story.

Now you've created your own hilarious MAD LIBS® game!

## MOM'S MESSAGES

NUMBER _____

PLURAL NOUN _____

NOUN _____

ADJECTIVE _____

NOUN _____

VERB (PAST TENSE) _____

VERB _____

NOUN _____

PART OF THE BODY _____

NOUN _____

NOUN _____

NOUN _____

SILLY WORD _____

NOUN _____

ADJECTIVE _____

# MAD LIBS®
# MOM'S MESSAGES

Hi, it's your mother. Where are you? I've left over _____
NUMBER

_____ on your answering _____. Maybe
PLURAL NOUN                                    NOUN

you forgot to turn the _____ ringer on. You're coming for
ADJECTIVE

_____ tonight, aren't you? You certainly could use a home-
NOUN

_____ meal. I'll call you later . . . Hello, it's me again. I'm at
VERB (PAST TENSE)

the doctor. Don't _____. I'm fine. I was in the market and I
VERB

slipped on a/an _____ peel. The doctor says I sprained my
NOUN

_____. I may have to wear a brace on the _____ or
PART OF THE BODY                                          NOUN

use crutches. But don't worry, honey. I'll call back . . . Hello? Good, you're finally

answering. What? I can't speak any louder. I'm seeing a/an _____
NOUN

at the theater. Shakespeare's *A Midsummer Night's* _____.
NOUN

_____! I'm going to have to lower my _____; the
SILLY WORD                                    NOUN

actors are giving me _____ looks. I'll call you back.
ADJECTIVE

MAD LIBS® is fun to play with friends, but you can also play it by yourself! To begin with, DO NOT look at the story on the page below. Fill in the blanks on this page with the words called for. Then, using the words you have selected, fill in the blank spaces in the story.

Now you've created your own hilarious MAD LIBS® game!

# E-MAIL FROM AN INSOMNIAC

ADJECTIVE _____

PLURAL NOUN _____

NOUN _____

PART OF THE BODY _____

NOUN _____

ADJECTIVE _____

ANIMAL _____

ADJECTIVE _____

NOUN _____

VERB ENDING IN "ING" _____

NOUN _____

ADJECTIVE _____

NOUN _____

PART OF THE BODY (PLURAL) _____

VERB _____

ADJECTIVE _____

PART OF THE BODY _____

# MAD LIBS®
# E-MAIL FROM AN INSOMNIAC

Fellow insomniacs, I have some _____ news to share with you!
ADJECTIVE

Last night, for the first time in many _____, I slept through
PLURAL NOUN

the entire _____. The minute my _____ hit the
NOUN                                    PART OF THE BODY

_____, I fell into a/an _____ sleep. Here are some
NOUN                                    ADJECTIVE

tips on how you can do it, too:

• Don't take _____ naps. They will keep you _____
ANIMAL                                                ADJECTIVE

at night.

• Don't eat a heavy _____ before _____ to bed.
NOUN                              VERB ENDING IN "ING"

• Take a hot _____ or a/an _____ shower before
NOUN                              ADJECTIVE

hitting the _____. It will relax all your _____.
NOUN                                      PART OF THE BODY (PLURAL)

• And most importantly, make sure you _____ in a comfortable
VERB

bed that offers _____ support for your _____.
ADJECTIVE                              PART OF THE BODY

From COOL MAD LIBS® • Copyright © 2001 by Penguin Random House LLC.

MAD LIBS® is fun to play with friends, but you can also play it by yourself! To begin with, DO NOT look at the story on the page below. Fill in the blanks on this page with the words called for. Then, using the words you have selected, fill in the blank spaces in the story.

Now you've created your own hilarious MAD LIBS® game!

# THE APPOINTMENT

ADJECTIVE _____

FIRST NAME (FEMALE) _____

NOUN _____

FIRST NAME (FEMALE) _____

NOUN _____

ADVERB _____

VERB ENDING IN "ING" _____

NOUN _____

NUMBER _____

NOUN _____

NOUN _____

NOUN _____

VERB (PAST TENSE) _____

NOUN _____

FIRST NAME (MALE) _____

PLURAL NOUN _____

# MAD LIBS®
# THE APPOINTMENT

(TO BE PERFORMED BY TWO _____ ACTORS)
ADJECTIVE

Receptionist: Good morning, _____'s Beauty and
FIRST NAME (FEMALE)

_____ Salon.
NOUN

Woman on phone: I'd like to make an appointment with _____
FIRST NAME (FEMALE)

to have my _____ colored and styled.
NOUN

Receptionist: Oh, I'm _____ sorry. She isn't in today. She had a/an
ADVERB

_____ accident and broke her _____ in
VERB ENDING IN "ING"  NOUN

_____ places.
NUMBER

Woman on phone: Oh my, that's terrible. Who can style my _____?
NOUN

I'm going to my daughter's _____ performance tonight. I can't
NOUN

possibly go without having my _____ done and my eyebrows
NOUN

_____. And I have just discovered a broken _____.
VERB (PAST TENSE)  NOUN

Receptionist: Relax, madam. _____ is the answer to all your
FIRST NAME (MALE)

_____.
PLURAL NOUN

MAD LIBS® is fun to play with friends, but you can also play it by yourself! To begin with, DO NOT look at the story on the page below. Fill in the blanks on this page with the words called for. Then, using the words you have selected, fill in the blank spaces in the story.

Now you've created your own hilarious MAD LIBS® game!

# IT'S MAGIC

NOUN _____

OCCUPATION (PLURAL) _____

NOUN _____

NOUN _____

NOUN _____

VERB ENDING IN "ING" _____

PART OF THE BODY _____

PLURAL NOUN _____

ADJECTIVE _____

ADJECTIVE _____

PART OF THE BODY _____

ADJECTIVE _____

ANIMAL _____

ADJECTIVE _____

ADVERB _____

# MAD LIBS®
# IT'S MAGIC

Ever since I was a little _____, I have loved watching
NOUN

_____ perform their _____ tricks. If you've never
OCCUPATION (PLURAL)                    NOUN

seen a magician pull a/an _____ out of a/an _____
NOUN                                        NOUN

or catch a/an _____ bullet in his _____, you've
VERB ENDING IN "ING"                 PART OF THE BODY

missed many of life's greatest _____. When I was seventeen, I gave
PLURAL NOUN

_____ thought to becoming an expert in _____
ADJECTIVE                                          ADJECTIVE

magic. I was desperate to prove that the _____ is quicker than
PART OF THE BODY

the eye. Unfortunately, I didn't have the _____ skills to do that.
ADJECTIVE

Today, I satisfy my craving for magic by going to Las Vegas and watching famous

magicians make a live _____ disappear into _____
ANIMAL                                      ADJECTIVE

air, and the casinos make my money disappear just as _____.
ADVERB

MAD LIBS® is fun to play with friends, but you can also play it by yourself! To begin with, DO NOT look at the story on the page below. Fill in the blanks on this page with the words called for. Then, using the words you have selected, fill in the blank spaces in the story.

Now you've created your own hilarious MAD LIBS® game!

# JOHNNY COOL, P.I., CHAPTER ONE

PERSON IN ROOM (MALE) _____

NOUN _____

NOUN _____

NOUN _____

NOUN _____

NOUN _____

NOUN _____

PART OF THE BODY _____

NOUN _____

NOUN _____

ADJECTIVE _____

ADJECTIVE _____

NOUN _____

NOUN _____

ADVERB _____

_____, alias Johnny Cool, hated to make decisions, even when
PERSON IN ROOM (MALE)

his _____ depended on it. He headed in the direction of an all-night
NOUN

_____ nestled between a self-service _____ station
NOUN                                              NOUN

and a/an _____ parlor. He pushed open the diner _____
NOUN                                                      NOUN

but didn't enter. The only streetlamp on the dark _____
NOUN

illuminated the fear on his _____. He was coming to another
PART OF THE BODY

decisive moment, and, as always, it scared the _____ out of
NOUN

him. He took a deep _____ and entered the diner. It was
NOUN

almost _____. Johnny slumped into a/an _____
ADJECTIVE                                              ADJECTIVE

leather booth. He was tired. Every _____ in his body ached. His
NOUN

_____ was trembling. He needed coffee _____.
NOUN                                               ADVERB

MAD LIBS® is fun to play with friends, but you can also play it by yourself! To begin with, DO NOT look at the story on the page below. Fill in the blanks on this page with the words called for. Then, using the words you have selected, fill in the blank spaces in the story.

Now you've created your own hilarious MAD LIBS® game!

# JOHNNY COOL, P.I., CHAPTER TWO

PLURAL NOUN _____

NOUN _____

COLOR _____

TYPE OF LIQUID_____

NOUN _____

VERB (PAST TENSE) _____

NOUN _____

NOUN _____

NOUN _____

PART OF THE BODY _____

ADJECTIVE _____

NOUN _____

PLURAL NOUN _____

NOUN _____

VERB ENDING IN "ING" _____

# MAD LIBS®
# JOHNNY COOL, P.I., CHAPTER TWO

Johnny Cool drummed his _____ on the _____
                        PLURAL NOUN                    NOUN

in the restaurant. The _____-haired waitress brought him a cup
                          COLOR

of steaming hot _____ and a grease-splattered _____.
                  TYPE OF LIQUID                                  NOUN

He _____ at the menu. The moment he'd been dreading
      VERB (PAST TENSE)

had come. Shivers ran up and down his _____. Beads of
                                          NOUN

_____ poured over his _____ and down his
      NOUN                            NOUN

_____. "Made up your mind?" asked the _____
   PART OF THE BODY                                    ADJECTIVE

waitress. Johnny reached for his voice, and in a barely audible _____
                                                                    NOUN

said, "Ham and scrambled _____." "Okay," said the waitress, writing
                            PLURAL NOUN

it down on her _____. "What kind of toast would you like—white
                   NOUN

or wheat?" Johnny Cool could not handle another decision. He ran out of the

diner, _____ at the top of his lungs.
          VERB ENDING IN "ING"

MAD LIBS® is fun to play with friends, but you can also play it by yourself! To begin with, DO NOT look at the story on the page below. Fill in the blanks on this page with the words called for. Then, using the words you have selected, fill in the blank spaces in the story.

Now you've created your own hilarious MAD LIBS® game!

# ICE-SKATING CHAMP

PERSON IN ROOM (FEMALE) _____

NOUN _____

ADJECTIVE _____

PART OF THE BODY (PLURAL) _____

ADJECTIVE _____

PLURAL NOUN _____

PLURAL NOUN _____

NOUN _____

NOUN _____

PLURAL NOUN _____

NOUN _____

LAST NAME_____

ADJECTIVE _____

ADJECTIVE _____

LAST NAME_____

NOUN _____

# MAD LIBS®

# ICE-SKATING CHAMP

Traditionally, _____ is as cool as the _____ on
PERSON IN ROOM (FEMALE)                                    NOUN

which she skates. Last night, however, she surprised her _____
                                                                ADJECTIVE

fans by pumping her _____ in the air and jumping into
                        PART OF THE BODY (PLURAL)

her _____ coach's _____ when her winning
        ADJECTIVE                     PLURAL NOUN

_____ were flashed on the _____! Once again,
    PLURAL NOUN                             NOUN

America's five-time _____ champion had outdueled her four
                          NOUN

_____ to win her third world _____. In a
    PLURAL NOUN                                       NOUN

postgame interview, her coach, Pops _____, justified the champ's
                                        LAST NAME

_____ enthusiasm: "Tonight she displayed _____
    ADJECTIVE                                                ADJECTIVE

athleticism in performing the triple _____ loop and the double
                                          LAST NAME

_____. I don't think she's ever been better!"
    NOUN

MAD LIBS® is fun to play with friends, but you can also play it by yourself! To begin with, DO NOT look at the story on the page below. Fill in the blanks on this page with the words called for. Then, using the words you have selected, fill in the blank spaces in the story.

Now you've created your own hilarious MAD LIBS® game!

# SNOWBOARDING INSTRUCTIONS

PERSON IN ROOM _____

OCCUPATION _____

VERB ENDING IN "ING" _____

PLURAL NOUN _____

ADJECTIVE _____

NOUN _____

ADJECTIVE _____

NOUN _____

ADVERB _____

PART OF THE BODY _____

PLURAL NOUN _____

NOUN _____

NOUN _____

ADVERB _____

ADJECTIVE _____

ADJECTIVE _____

NUMBER _____

NOUN _____

ADJECTIVE _____

# MAD LIBS®
# SNOWBOARDING INSTRUCTIONS

Good morning, everyone. I am _____, your snowboarding
                                    PERSON IN ROOM

_____. How many of you have gone _____
        OCCUPATION                                      VERB ENDING IN "ING"

before? Please raise your _____. None of you? Well, I feel
                                PLURAL NOUN

I must warn you that while snowboarding is _____ fun, it is
                                                    ADJECTIVE

also a dangerous _____ and is much more difficult than skiing
                        NOUN

at first. This may come as a/an _____ surprise to you. But take
                                        ADJECTIVE

a/an _____ to think about it. When you ski, your weight is
            NOUN

_____ distributed. You have one _____ on each ski,
        ADVERB                                      PART OF THE BODY

helping you maintain your balance. Snowboarding requires you to keep both of

your _____ on a narrow _____. Maintaining your
            PLURAL NOUN                        NOUN

_____ is _____ hard. However, I promise if you
        NOUN                ADVERB

are a/an _____ learner and pay _____ attention,
                ADJECTIVE                            ADJECTIVE

I will have you executing a/an _____-degree _____
                                        NUMBER                        NOUN

grab within one _____ week.
                        ADJECTIVE

MAD LIBS® is fun to play with friends, but you can also play it by yourself! To begin with, DO NOT look at the story on the page below. Fill in the blanks on this page with the words called for. Then, using the words you have selected, fill in the blank spaces in the story.

Now you've created your own hilarious MAD LIBS® game!

## MOON FACTS

ADJECTIVE _____

NOUN _____

NOUN _____

ADJECTIVE _____

PLURAL NOUN _____

NOUN _____

NUMBER _____

NOUN _____

SAME NOUN _____

PERSON IN ROOM _____

PERSON IN ROOM _____

NOUN _____

PLURAL NOUN _____

PART OF THE BODY _____

PLURAL NOUN _____

ADJECTIVE _____

NOUN _____

# MAD LIBS®
# MOON FACTS

- Even though the moon first appears as a/an _____ slice of
  ADJECTIVE

  light and finally becomes a full _____, it doesn't change its
  NOUN

  _____. The moon looks different as the _____ sun
  NOUN                                                ADJECTIVE

  illuminates its different _____.
  PLURAL NOUN

- The moon rotates around the _____ once every _____ days.
  NOUN                                         NUMBER

- If the moon were to be seen next to the Earth, it would look like a tennis

  _____ next to a bowling _____.
  NOUN                                 SAME NOUN

- In 1969, _____ and _____ from the Apollo
  PERSON IN ROOM        PERSON IN ROOM

  _____ were the first human _____ to set
  NOUN                                     PLURAL NOUN

  _____ on the moon. Many historians and _____
  PART OF THE BODY                                     PLURAL NOUN

  believe this to be the most _____ achievement in the history of
  ADJECTIVE

  the _____.
  NOUN

MAD LIBS® is fun to play with friends, but you can also play it by yourself! To begin with, DO NOT look at the story on the page below. Fill in the blanks on this page with the words called for. Then, using the words you have selected, fill in the blank spaces in the story.

Now you've created your own hilarious MAD LIBS® game!

## OFF THE EYE CHART

VERB ENDING IN "ING" _____

ADJECTIVE _____

NOUN _____

NOUN _____

SILLY WORD _____

PLURAL NOUN _____

NOUN _____

NOUN _____

PLURAL NOUN _____

PLURAL NOUN _____

NOUN _____

ADJECTIVE _____

PLURAL NOUN _____

ADVERB _____

# MAD LIBS®
# OFF THE EYE CHART

(DIALOGUE BETWEEN PATIENT AND EYE DOCTOR IN DOCTOR'S OFFICE)

Patient: Thanks for _____ me into your _____
VERB ENDING IN "ING"                    ADJECTIVE

schedule. I have to go on tour in the morning.

Doctor: Are you a rock _____?
NOUN

Patient: Yes. I'm the lead _____ with the _____ band.
NOUN                              SILLY WORD

Doctor: What kind of problems are you having with your _____?
PLURAL NOUN

Patient: When I try to read my _____ music, I have trouble with
NOUN

the small _____.
NOUN

Doctor: Have you ever worn eye _____ or contact _____?
PLURAL NOUN                          PLURAL NOUN

Patient: Just _____ glasses.
NOUN

Doctor: Let's test your eyes. Look at the chart. When do the letters become

_____?
ADJECTIVE

Patient: What chart, Doc?

Doctor: The large one with _____. Right in front of you . . . on the wall.
PLURAL NOUN

Patient: What wall?

Doctor: You _____ need glasses!
ADVERB

MAD LIBS® is fun to play with friends, but you can also play it by yourself! To begin with, DO NOT look at the story on the page below. Fill in the blanks on this page with the words called for. Then, using the words you have selected, fill in the blank spaces in the story.

Now you've created your own hilarious MAD LIBS® game!

# WORD GAMES

PLURAL NOUN _____

NOUN _____

NOUN _____

ADJECTIVE _____

VERB _____

PLURAL NOUN _____

PLURAL NOUN _____

PLURAL NOUN _____

VERB _____

ADJECTIVE _____

ADJECTIVE _____

SAME ADJECTIVE _____

VERB _____

VERB ENDING IN "ING" _____

SAME ADJECTIVE _____

PLURAL NOUN _____

In the early 1900s, crossword _____ only appeared in children's
PLURAL NOUN

books. Today, _____ puzzles are in almost every _____
NOUN                                                                          NOUN

printed in the US and throughout the whole _____ world. More
ADJECTIVE

people do crossword puzzles than _____ or drink _____.
VERB                                        PLURAL NOUN

Some fanatics are known to do their puzzles even before they wash their

_____, brush their _____, or _____
PLURAL NOUN                          PLURAL NOUN                      VERB

their breakfasts in the morning. Another _____ word game
ADJECTIVE

is _____ Libs. Not only is _____ Libs fun to
ADJECTIVE                               SAME ADJECTIVE

_____, but it is also an informative _____ tool.
VERB                                                  VERB ENDING IN "ING"

By playing _____ Libs, kids learn how to use nouns, adjectives,
SAME ADJECTIVE

adverbs, and _____.
PLURAL NOUN

MAD LIBS® is fun to play with friends, but you can also play it by yourself! To begin with, DO NOT look at the story on the page below. Fill in the blanks on this page with the words called for. Then, using the words you have selected, fill in the blank spaces in the story.

Now you've created your own hilarious MAD LIBS® game!

# SNOWED IN

NOUN _____

ADVERB _____

PLURAL NOUN _____

NOUN _____

PLURAL NOUN _____

NOUN _____

PLURAL NOUN _____

NOUN _____

ADJECTIVE _____

PLURAL NOUN _____

PLURAL NOUN _____

ADJECTIVE _____

PLURAL NOUN _____

ADJECTIVE _____

NOUN _____

NOUN _____

# MAD LIBS®
## SNOWED IN

If you can't get out of your house because of a sudden _____-storm,

NOUN

don't panic. You'll be _____ safe if you have the following

ADVERB

_____ on hand:

PLURAL NOUN

• At least one flash-_____ in working condition with plenty of

NOUN

extra _____

PLURAL NOUN

• A/An _____-operated radio that receives both AM and CB

NOUN

_____

PLURAL NOUN

• A first-aid _____

NOUN

• A week's supply of _____ water

ADJECTIVE

• Warm clothes. Preferably woolen _____, thermal _____,

PLURAL NOUN          PLURAL NOUN

and, of course, _____ underwear

ADJECTIVE

• Emergency numbers for the police and fire _____, your

PLURAL NOUN

_____ doctor, and a close _____ member posted

ADJECTIVE                      NOUN

in a convenient _____

NOUN

MAD LIBS® is fun to play with friends, but you can also play it by yourself! To begin with, DO NOT look at the story on the page below. Fill in the blanks on this page with the words called for. Then, using the words you have selected, fill in the blank spaces in the story.

Now you've created your own hilarious MAD LIBS® game!

## PENGUIN FACTS

PLURAL NOUN _____

LAST NAME _____

NOUN _____

PLURAL NOUN _____

ADVERB _____

VERB _____

ADJECTIVE _____

PART OF THE BODY (PLURAL) _____

PLURAL NOUN _____

VERB _____

NOUN _____

NOUN _____

PART OF THE BODY (PLURAL) _____

ADJECTIVE _____

PLURAL NOUN _____

PLURAL NOUN _____

# MAD LIBS®
# PENGUIN FACTS

Fellow bird _____, we are honored to have as our speaker today
PLURAL NOUN

Dr. _____, America's foremost _____ on penguins
LAST NAME                                                  NOUN

and other cold-climate _____.The doctor has _____
PLURAL NOUN                                          ADVERB

agreed to answer three questions before we _____ for lunch.
VERB

Doctor: First question, please.

Question: Why do penguins walk in such a/an _____ way?
ADJECTIVE

Doctor: You'd walk funny, too, if every step you took put your

_____ on frozen _____. Next!
PART OF THE BODY (PLURAL)          PLURAL NOUN

Question: How do penguins manage to _____ in such a cold
VERB

_____?
NOUN

Doctor: They have an abundance of _____ under their
NOUN

_____. This fat insulates them against _____
PART OF THE BODY (PLURAL)                                      ADJECTIVE

weather. Next!

Question: Why do we only see black-and-white penguins?

Doctor: Because they're very formal _____. They dress for all
PLURAL NOUN

occasions, especially sit-down _____.
PLURAL NOUN

MAD LIBS® is fun to play with friends, but you can also play it by yourself! To begin with, DO NOT look at the story on the page below. Fill in the blanks on this page with the words called for. Then, using the words you have selected, fill in the blank spaces in the story.

Now you've created your own hilarious MAD LIBS® game!

# CLOSE DANCING IS COOL...AGAIN

VERB ENDING IN "ING" _____

PLURAL NOUN _____

ADJECTIVE _____

PLURAL NOUN _____

SAME PLURAL NOUN _____

SAME PLURAL NOUN _____

PLURAL NOUN _____

NOUN _____

NOUN _____

PLURAL NOUN _____

PLURAL NOUN _____

PART OF THE BODY (PLURAL) _____

ADVERB _____

NUMBER _____

PLURAL NOUN _____

PART OF THE BODY _____

ADJECTIVE _____

# MAD LIBS®
## CLOSE DANCING IS COOL ... AGAIN

The waltz, the merengue, swing, and ballroom _____ are making
                                             VERB ENDING IN "ING"

a comeback with kids of all _____. A recent study shows a/an
                            PLURAL NOUN

_____ percentage of students in elementary _____,
ADJECTIVE                                                 PLURAL NOUN

middle _____, and even high _____ are dropping
       SAME PLURAL NOUN                   SAME PLURAL NOUN

their Phys Ed _____ in golf, bowling, and _____-Pong
              PLURAL NOUN                              NOUN

to take up _____ dancing. Close dancing, in which partners hold
           NOUN

each other's _____ and put their _____ around
             PLURAL NOUN                      PLURAL NOUN

each other's _____, is considered _____
             PART OF THE BODY (PLURAL)          ADVERB

cool these days. Sociologists predict that within the next _____
                                                           NUMBER

years, almost all teen _____ will once again be dancing cheek to
                       PLURAL NOUN

_____ to the sound of a/an _____ band.
PART OF THE BODY                        ADJECTIVE

MAD LIBS® is fun to play with friends, but you can also play it by yourself! To begin with, DO NOT look at the story on the page below. Fill in the blanks on this page with the words called for. Then, using the words you have selected, fill in the blank spaces in the story.

Now you've created your own hilarious MAD LIBS® game!

# TELEVISION PITCH FOR A BOOK ON HOW TO OVERCOME SHYNESS

NOUN _____

PART OF THE BODY _____

PLURAL NOUN _____

NOUN _____

NOUN _____

NOUN _____

ADVERB _____

ADVERB _____

NUMBER _____

NOUN _____

NOUN _____

PLURAL NOUN _____

VERB _____

ADVERB _____

NOUN _____

OCCUPATION (PLURAL)_____

# MAD LIBS®
## TELEVISION PITCH FOR A BOOK ON HOW TO OVERCOME SHYNESS

(TO BE READ WITH GREAT SINCERITY)

Are you unable to introduce yourself to a member of the opposite

_____ without becoming red in the _____?
　　　NOUN　　　　　　　　　　　　　　　　　　　　PART OF THE BODY

Are you uncomfortable in the presence of _____? Are you too
　　　　　　　　　　　　　　　　　　　　PLURAL NOUN

shy to raise your _____ in class when you have to go to the
　　　　　　　　　　NOUN

_____? If you answered no to all of the above, you are one cool
　　NOUN

_____. However, if you answered yes to any one of the questions, you
　　NOUN

are _____ shy and _____ in need of the nation's number
　　　ADVERB　　　　　　　　　ADVERB

_____ best-selling book, *Shyness Is a State of* _____.
　　NUMBER　　　　　　　　　　　　　　　　　　　　　　　　　NOUN

You can order this remarkable book by writing to the address now showing on

your TV _____. Send no _____. Just _____
　　　　　NOUN　　　　　　　　　PLURAL NOUN　　　　　　　VERB

later. If you can't wait to say bye to shy, call our toll-free number and we will rush

the book to you _____ at no extra _____. Call
　　　　　　　　ADVERB　　　　　　　　　　　NOUN

now; _____ are standing by.
　　OCCUPATION (PLURAL)

MAD LIBS® is fun to play with friends, but you can also play it by yourself! To begin with, DO NOT look at the story on the page below. Fill in the blanks on this page with the words called for. Then, using the words you have selected, fill in the blank spaces in the story.

Now you've created your own hilarious MAD LIBS® game!

# IGLOO FACTS

NOUN _____

NOUN _____

NOUN _____

PLURAL NOUN _____

PLURAL NOUN _____

NOUN _____

ADJECTIVE _____

PART OF THE BODY (PLURAL) _____

PART OF THE BODY (PLURAL) _____

ADVERB _____

ADJECTIVE _____

PLURAL NOUN _____

NOUN _____

VERB _____

VERB _____

NOUN _____

# MAD LIBS®
# IGLOO FACTS

An igloo is an Eskimo _____ or hut that is made from blocks
                              NOUN

of hard-packed _____. A well-built _____
                      NOUN                                    NOUN

not only provides comfort and warmth, but is also capable of withstanding

freezing _____ and howling _____. In bygone
              PLURAL NOUN                      PLURAL NOUN

years, if Eskimos traveling across a frozen _____ ran into a/an
                                                  NOUN

_____ snowstorm, one in which they couldn't see their
      ADJECTIVE

_____ in front of their _____, they
PART OF THE BODY (PLURAL)                   PART OF THE BODY (PLURAL)

would come to an abrupt stop and _____ construct an igloo.
                                          ADVERB

It took them almost a/an _____ day to build one. Today,
                              ADJECTIVE

with modern _____, an igloo can be completed in less than
                PLURAL NOUN

a/an _____. And if you have enough food to eat, water to
          NOUN

_____, and candles to _____, you can stay put and
      VERB                              VERB

safe for the rest of your _____.
                                NOUN

MAD LIBS® is fun to play with friends, but you can also play it by yourself! To begin with, DO NOT look at the story on the page below. Fill in the blanks on this page with the words called for. Then, using the words you have selected, fill in the blank spaces in the story.

Now you've created your own hilarious MAD LIBS® game!

## A RECIPE FOR ICE CUBES

ADJECTIVE _____

NOUN _____

NOUN _____

VERB _____

TYPE OF LIQUID_____

TYPE OF LIQUID_____

TYPE OF LIQUID_____

COLOR _____

VERB _____

VERB _____

NUMBER _____

ADJECTIVE _____

ADVERB _____

PART OF THE BODY (PLURAL) _____

VERB _____

VERB _____

# MAD LIBS®
# A RECIPE FOR ICE CUBES

To make _____ ice cubes, first find a tray with molds shaped like a/an
          ADJECTIVE

_____ or a/an _____. Then _____
      NOUN                      NOUN                      VERB

once while holding the tray. Fill the molds with _____, or even
                                                  TYPE OF LIQUID

_____, but for the best results always use _____. It
  TYPE OF LIQUID                                        TYPE OF LIQUID

can even be dyed _____ if you wish. _____ carefully when
                      COLOR                          VERB

placing the tray in the freezer. Allow the cubes to _____ for at least
                                                         VERB

_____ minutes until they are completely _____. Remove
    NUMBER                                              ADJECTIVE

the tray _____, and jiggle with your _____ until the
             ADVERB                              PART OF THE BODY (PLURAL)

cubes _____. Add to your favorite drink and _____!
          VERB                                              VERB

# MAD LIBS®

## HOLLY, JOLLY MAD LIBS

MAD LIBS® is fun to play with friends, but you can also play it by yourself! To begin with, DO NOT look at the story on the page below. Fill in the blanks on this page with the words called for. Then, using the words you have selected, fill in the blank spaces in the story.

Now you've created your own hilarious MAD LIBS® game!

## VISIT THE NORTH POLE!

ADJECTIVE _____

ADJECTIVE _____

NOUN _____

ADVERB _____

ADJECTIVE _____

PART OF THE BODY (PLURAL) _____

NOUN _____

PLURAL NOUN _____

NOUN _____

ADJECTIVE _____

ADJECTIVE _____

ADJECTIVE _____

PLURAL NOUN _____

ADJECTIVE _____

PART OF THE BODY _____

PLURAL NOUN _____

# MAD LIBS®
# VISIT THE NORTH POLE!

Looking for a/an _____ destination for your next vacation?
ADJECTIVE

How about the _____ North Pole? Located in the middle of the
ADJECTIVE

Arctic _____, it is made up of _____ shifting ice,
NOUN                                    ADVERB

which makes it perfect for snowshoeing through the _____
                                                    ADJECTIVE

tundra. As you trek across the ice, keep your _____ peeled
                                              PART OF THE BODY (PLURAL)

for the incredible wildlife that inhabits the North _____—like
                                                      NOUN

furry white polar _____, _____ seals, and
                   PLURAL NOUN        NOUN

_____ arctic foxes. And when night falls you are in for a/an
ADJECTIVE

_____ treat. You'll be able to see the _____ aurora
ADJECTIVE                                          ADJECTIVE

borealis, otherwise known as the northern _____. This incredible
                                            PLURAL NOUN

display of _____ lights will blow your _____. So
            ADJECTIVE                              PART OF THE BODY

call 1-800-555-3939 and make your travel _____ today!
                                          PLURAL NOUN

MAD LIBS® is fun to play with friends, but you can also play it by yourself! To begin with, DO NOT look at the story on the page below. Fill in the blanks on this page with the words called for. Then, using the words you have selected, fill in the blank spaces in the story.

Now you've created your own hilarious MAD LIBS® game!

# SANTA BLOG

ADJECTIVE _____

ADJECTIVE _____

NOUN _____

ADJECTIVE _____

A PLACE _____

NOUN _____

PLURAL NOUN _____

PLURAL NOUN _____

ADVERB _____

NOUN _____

ADJECTIVE _____

VERB _____

VERB _____

ADJECTIVE _____

ADJECTIVE _____

PLURAL NOUN _____

# MAD LIBS®
# SANTA BLOG

Ho, ho, ho, _____ blog fans! Santa here. It's crunch time
ADJECTIVE

at my _____ workshop, and everyone is as busy as a/an
ADJECTIVE

_____. I've received tons of _____ letters
NOUN                                          ADJECTIVE

from girls and boys around (the) _____, and the elves
A PLACE

have been working round the _____ to make all of their
NOUN

_____. Plus, I've finally finished putting together the list of
PLURAL NOUN

naughty _____, which I'm _____ happy to
PLURAL NOUN                      ADVERB

say is much shorter than last year's! As I look out the _____, I
NOUN

can see the reindeer are groomed and look really _____, and
ADJECTIVE

my sleigh is polished and ready to _____. I will be able to
VERB

_____ through the _____ night sky as soon as
VERB                            ADJECTIVE

Mrs. Claus finishes letting out my _____ red suit. I'm sorry to say,
ADJECTIVE

I ate a few too many _____ this past year!
PLURAL NOUN

See you soon,

Santa

MAD LIBS® is fun to play with friends, but you can also play it by yourself! To begin with, DO NOT look at the story on the page below. Fill in the blanks on this page with the words called for. Then, using the words you have selected, fill in the blank spaces in the story.

Now you've created your own hilarious MAD LIBS® game!

## HOLIDAY WEATHER REPORT

ADJECTIVE _____

PERSON IN ROOM _____

NOUN _____

ADJECTIVE _____

ADJECTIVE _____

NUMBER _____

NOUN _____

NOUN _____

PLURAL NOUN _____

PLURAL NOUN _____

VERB ENDING IN "ING" _____

NUMBER _____

ADJECTIVE _____

PLURAL NOUN _____

VERB _____

NOUN _____

NOUN _____

ADJECTIVE _____

# MAD LIBS®
# HOLIDAY WEATHER REPORT

Good evening, and _____ holidays. I'm _____
 ADJECTIVE                                      PERSON IN ROOM

with your local weather _____. First the good news: We're going
                               NOUN

to have a traditional _____ Christmas. A/An _____
                              ADJECTIVE                              ADJECTIVE

snowstorm is heading our way. You can expect three to _____ feet
                                                              NUMBER

of _____ to accumulate before the end of this _____,
       NOUN                                                          NOUN

plus several more _____ of snow by midnight. And you may
                        PLURAL NOUN

want to put on your warm _____: Overnight, the temperature
                                PLURAL NOUN

is going to drop below _____ level, with a windchill of
                          VERB ENDING IN "ING"

negative _____ degrees. Now the bad news: Driving conditions
              NUMBER

will be extremely _____. I strongly suggest you stay off the
                        ADJECTIVE

_____ and _____ at home. Hunker down, light
   PLURAL NOUN                   VERB

a/an _____ in the fireplace, and watch the _____-flakes
         NOUN                                                 NOUN

fall. And most importantly, have a/an _____ Christmas!
                                            ADJECTIVE

MAD LIBS® is fun to play with friends, but you can also play it by yourself! To begin with, DO NOT look at the story on the page below. Fill in the blanks on this page with the words called for. Then, using the words you have selected, fill in the blank spaces in the story.

Now you've created your own hilarious MAD LIBS® game!

## MOST POPULAR GIFTS

ADJECTIVE _____

PLURAL NOUN _____

NOUN _____

ADJECTIVE _____

PLURAL NOUN _____

NOUN _____

NOUN _____

NOUN _____

NOUN _____

NOUN _____

ADJECTIVE _____

NOUN _____

PLURAL NOUN _____

ADJECTIVE _____

NOUN _____

ADJECTIVE _____

NOUN _____

NOUN _____

A_____

N_____

# MAD LIBS®
# MOST POPULAR GIFTS

Here is a list of the most _____ gifts for your dear _____:
ADJECTIVE                                                        PLURAL NOUN

5. An i-_____. This _____ device can store and play
NOUN                    ADJECTIVE

up to thirty thousand _____.
PLURAL NOUN

4. A/An _____-cam. Shoot movies or film yourself acting like a/an
NOUN

_____. Then, upload your videos to You-_____,
NOUN                                                      NOUN

where everyone can see them!

3. *Rock* _____. Ever wanted to be a famous _____?
NOUN                                              NOUN

You can act like one with this _____ video game.
ADJECTIVE

2. A flat-screen _____. Watch your favorite movies and TV
NOUN

_____ in _____-definition on an LCD _____.
PLURAL NOUN        ADJECTIVE                            NOUN

1. If you have _____ friends who are in short supply of
ADJECTIVE

self-esteem, buy them a talking _____. With the push of a/an
NOUN

_____, it will say things like, "You're so _____!" and
NOUN                                               ADJECTIVE

"You're the best _____ ever!"
NOUN

MAD LIBS® is fun to play with friends, but you can also play it by yourself! To begin with, DO NOT look at the story on the page below. Fill in the blanks on this page with the words called for. Then, using the words you have selected, fill in the blank spaces in the story.

Now you've created your own hilarious MAD LIBS® game!

# TAKING CARE OF YOUR REINDEER

ADJECTIVE _____

ADJECTIVE _____

NOUN _____

ADJECTIVE _____

NUMBER _____

ADJECTIVE _____

PLURAL NOUN _____

ADJECTIVE _____

NOUN _____

ADJECTIVE _____

NUMBER _____

ADVERB _____

ADJECTIVE _____

NOUN _____

NOUN _____

ADVERB _____

ADJECTIVE _____

# MAD LIBS®
# TAKING CARE OF YOUR REINDEER

Congratulations! We hear you've adopted a/an _____ reindeer.
ADJECTIVE

They make _____ pets—but they require a lot of care and
ADJECTIVE

_____. Here are some tips for keeping your reindeer happy and
NOUN

_____:
ADJECTIVE

• Feed it _____ times a day. Not difficult to do, as reindeer have a
NUMBER

very _____ diet. They eat grasses, moss, and _____.
ADJECTIVE     PLURAL NOUN

• Make sure your reindeer gets _____ exercise. In the wild,
ADJECTIVE

they travel farther than any other land _____. They go on
NOUN

_____ migrations, sometimes covering _____ miles.
ADJECTIVE     NUMBER

• Groom your reindeer _____. Its _____ antlers
ADVERB     ADJECTIVE

are covered in delicate _____, which you can clean with a soft
NOUN

_____. You should also brush its coat _____ once a month.
NOUN     ADVERB

• Take your reindeer to the vet often to make sure it stays healthy and

_____.
ADJECTIVE

MAD LIBS® is fun to play with friends, but you can also play it by yourself! To begin with, DO NOT look at the story on the page below. Fill in the blanks on this page with the words called for. Then, using the words you have selected, fill in the blank spaces in the story.

Now you've created your own hilarious MAD LIBS® game!

## GET TO KNOW MRS. CLAUS

ADJECTIVE _____

NOUN _____

FIRST NAME _____

NOUN _____

LAST NAME_____

ADJECTIVE _____

PLURAL NOUN _____

PLURAL NOUN _____

NOUN _____

NOUN _____

NOUN _____

NOUN _____

PART OF THE BODY (PLURAL) _____

ADJECTIVE _____

ADJECTIVE _____

ADJECTIVE _____

# MAD LIBS®
# GET TO KNOW MRS. CLAUS

Here are some _____ facts you may not know about me, Santa
<br>ADJECTIVE

Claus's dear _____:
<br>NOUN

Full name: Mrs. _____ Claus
<br>FIRST NAME

Hometown: The North _____
<br>NOUN

Activities: Helping my husband, Santa _____, get ready for
<br>LAST NAME

Christmas and taking care of the _____ elves
<br>ADJECTIVE

Interests: Baking Christmas _____ and knitting cozy _____
<br>PLURAL NOUN — PLURAL NOUN

Favorite Movies: *It's a Wonderful* _____, *Rudolph the Red-Nosed*
<br>NOUN

_____
<br>NOUN

Favorite Books: *The* _____ *Before Christmas, How the*
<br>NOUN

_____ *Stole Christmas*
<br>NOUN

Favorite Quotation: "All I want for Christmas is my two front

_____."
<br>PART OF THE BODY (PLURAL)

About Me: Have you ever wondered who brings _____ Santa
<br>ADJECTIVE

*his* _____ gifts on Christmas Eve? Well, surprise! It's little,
<br>ADJECTIVE

_____ me!
<br>ADJECTIVE

MAD LIBS® is fun to play with friends, but you can also play it by yourself! To begin with, DO NOT look at the story on the page below. Fill in the blanks on this page with the words called for. Then, using the words you have selected, fill in the blank spaces in the story.

Now you've created your own hilarious MAD LIBS® game!

## CHRISTMAS FUNNIES, PART 1

ADJECTIVE _____

ADJECTIVE _____

ADJECTIVE _____

NOUN _____

NOUN _____

ADJECTIVE _____

NOUN _____

PLURAL NOUN _____

Q: What do you get when you cross a/an _____ vampire with
                                              ADJECTIVE

a/an _____ snowman?
          ADJECTIVE

A: Frostbite!


Q: Why did the _____ reindeer cross the _____?
                      ADJECTIVE                              NOUN

A: To get to the other _____!
                              NOUN


Q: What do _____ elves sing to Santa?
                  ADJECTIVE

A: "*Freeze* a Jolly Good _____."
                                    NOUN


Q: What do polar _____ eat for lunch?
                      PLURAL NOUN

A: *Iceberg*-ers!

MAD LIBS® is fun to play with friends, but you can also play it by yourself! To begin with, DO NOT look at the story on the page below. Fill in the blanks on this page with the words called for. Then, using the words you have selected, fill in the blank spaces in the story.

Now you've created your own hilarious MAD LIBS® game!

## CHRISTMAS FUNNIES, PART 2

ADJECTIVE _____

FIRST NAME _____

PERSON IN ROOM _____

ADJECTIVE _____

TYPE OF ANIMAL (PLURAL) _____

PLURAL NOUN _____

SAME PLURAL NOUN _____

# MAD LIBS®
# CHRISTMAS FUNNIES, PART 2

Q: What do you call a/an _____ person who is afraid of
ADJECTIVE

_____ Claus?
FIRST NAME

A: *Claus*trophobic.

Q: What happened when _____ ate all the Christmas decorations?
PERSON IN ROOM

A: He/She caught a/an _____ case of *tinsel*-itis!
ADJECTIVE

Q: What do wild _____ sing at Christmas?
TYPE OF ANIMAL (PLURAL)

A: *Jungle* _____, *jungle* _____, *jungle* all the way!
PLURAL NOUN                          SAME PLURAL NOUN

MAD LIBS® is fun to play with friends, but you can also play it by yourself! To begin with, DO NOT look at the story on the page below. Fill in the blanks on this page with the words called for. Then, using the words you have selected, fill in the blank spaces in the story.

Now you've created your own hilarious MAD LIBS® game!

# CHRISTMAS AROUND THE WORLD, PART 1

ADJECTIVE _____

PLURAL NOUN _____

NOUN _____

ADJECTIVE _____

PLURAL NOUN _____

ADVERB _____

NOUN _____

NOUN _____

NOUN _____

PLURAL NOUN _____

PLURAL NOUN _____

ADJECTIVE _____

ADJECTIVE _____

ADJECTIVE _____

PLURAL NOUN _____

PLURAL NOUN _____

PLURAL NOUN _____

Americans have many _____ Christmas traditions. They decorate
ADJECTIVE

Christmas _____, sing _____ carols, and have
PLURAL NOUN                    NOUN

_____ Christmas dinners with their families. But how do
ADJECTIVE

_____ around the world celebrate?
PLURAL NOUN

- In Sweden, they _____ celebrate San Lucia Day before
ADVERB

Christmas. The youngest _____ in the family wears a
NOUN

white _____, a red _____, and a crown of
NOUN                        NOUN

_____ with candles in it. She then serves coffee and
PLURAL NOUN

_____ to everyone in her _____ family.
PLURAL NOUN                        ADJECTIVE

- In Australia, it is hot and _____ at Christmastime, because
ADJECTIVE

this _____ holiday falls in the middle of their summer.
ADJECTIVE

_____ gather outside at night to light _____ and
PLURAL NOUN                                        PLURAL NOUN

sing Christmas _____.
PLURAL NOUN

MAD LIBS® is fun to play with friends, but you can also play it by yourself! To begin with, DO NOT look at the story on the page below. Fill in the blanks on this page with the words called for. Then, using the words you have selected, fill in the blank spaces in the story.

Now you've created your own hilarious MAD LIBS® game!

# CHRISTMAS AROUND THE WORLD, PART 2

ADJECTIVE _____

PLURAL NOUN _____

ADJECTIVE _____

ADJECTIVE _____

PLURAL NOUN _____

PLURAL NOUN _____

ADJECTIVE _____

PLURAL NOUN _____

ADJECTIVE _____

NOUN _____

PLURAL NOUN _____

NOUN _____

NOUN _____

NOUN _____

PLURAL NOUN _____

# MAD LIBS®
# CHRISTMAS AROUND THE WORLD, PART 2

- In China, people decorate their _____ homes with paper
  <br>ADJECTIVE

  _____. They also put up _____ trees decorated with
  <br>PLURAL NOUN           ADJECTIVE

  _____ lanterns, _____, and red _____.
  <br>ADJECTIVE        PLURAL NOUN       PLURAL NOUN

- In Mexico, children look forward to a/an _____ party where
  <br>ADJECTIVE

  young _____ take turns hitting a/an _____ piñata
  <br>PLURAL NOUN         ADJECTIVE

  with a/an _____, until all the _____ and other
  <br>NOUN           PLURAL NOUN

  treats fall out.

- In Germany, families celebrate the weeks leading up to Christmas with an

  Advent _____. Each Sunday, they light another _____
  <br>NOUN           NOUN

  in the wreath. Before Christmas, Germans celebrate St. Nicholas Day, where kids

  put a/an _____ outside their door at night, and in the morning it
  <br>NOUN

  is filled with candy and _____.
  <br>PLURAL NOUN

MAD LIBS® is fun to play with friends, but you can also play it by yourself! To begin with, DO NOT look at the story on the page below. Fill in the blanks on this page with the words called for. Then, using the words you have selected, fill in the blank spaces in the story.

Now you've created your own hilarious MAD LIBS® game!

# A TROPICAL CHRISTMAS

PLURAL NOUN _____

NOUN _____

A PLACE _____

PLURAL NOUN _____

ADJECTIVE _____

NOUN _____

NOUN _____

PLURAL NOUN _____

ADJECTIVE _____

ADJECTIVE _____

PLURAL NOUN _____

ADJECTIVE _____

NOUN _____

ADJECTIVE _____

NOUN _____

NOUN _____

ADJECTIVE _____

# MAD LIBS®
# A TROPICAL CHRISTMAS

Some _____ can't imagine celebrating Christmas where
      PLURAL NOUN

there's no snow falling from the _____. But it's not all bad! Here
      NOUN

in (the) _____, where it's always sunny, we decorate palm
      A PLACE

_____ with _____ lights instead of decorating
   PLURAL NOUN        ADJECTIVE

a pine _____. Instead of making a snow-_____, we
     NOUN              NOUN

make _____ out of sand. Best of all, we don't have to bundle up
    PLURAL NOUN

against the _____ wind and the _____ cold and
      ADJECTIVE           ADJECTIVE

freeze our _____ off. At Christmas, we happily splash around in
     PLURAL NOUN

the _____ ocean and bask in the _____-shine.
    ADJECTIVE             NOUN

Or we go surfing and catch _____ waves. As you can see, I no
          ADJECTIVE

longer dream of a white _____. I'm happy celebrating Christmas
       NOUN

on a sandy _____ in the _____ sun!
     NOUN        ADJECTIVE

MAD LIBS® is fun to play with friends, but you can also play it by yourself! To begin with, DO NOT look at the story on the page below. Fill in the blanks on this page with the words called for. Then, using the words you have selected, fill in the blank spaces in the story.

Now you've created your own hilarious MAD LIBS® game!

# CHRISTMAS IN JULY

LAST NAME _____

ADJECTIVE _____

A PLACE _____

NOUN _____

PLURAL NOUN _____

ADVERB _____

NUMBER _____

ADJECTIVE _____

NOUN _____

NOUN _____

PLURAL NOUN _____

ADJECTIVE _____

VERB _____

NOUN _____

# MAD LIBS®
# CHRISTMAS IN JULY

Hurry on down to _____ Furniture for our _____
                        LAST NAME                              ADJECTIVE

Christmas-in-July sale! Yes, folks, Christmas has come early here in (the)

_____, and we're celebrating with _____-wide savings
     A PLACE                                         NOUN

on couches, tables, and _____! With prices _____
                          PLURAL NOUN                        ADVERB

reduced up to _____ percent off, you can't afford to miss this
                  NUMBER

_____ event! Purchase any _____ in the store with no
  ADJECTIVE                              NOUN

down _____ and no _____ for twelve months.
        NOUN                    PLURAL NOUN

But our _____ sale only lasts through Thursday. So don't delay!
           ADJECTIVE

_____ on down today, and have a merry _____
     VERB                                              NOUN

in July!

MAD LIBS® is fun to play with friends, but you can also play it by yourself! To begin with, DO NOT look at the story on the page below. Fill in the blanks on this page with the words called for. Then, using the words you have selected, fill in the blank spaces in the story.

Now you've created your own hilarious MAD LIBS® game!

# ELVES WANTED

PLURAL NOUN _____

NUMBER _____

ADJECTIVE _____

VERB _____

NOUN _____

PLURAL NOUN _____

NOUN _____

ADJECTIVE _____

NOUN _____

ADJECTIVE _____

ADJECTIVE _____

VERB _____

PLURAL NOUN _____

A PLACE _____

PART OF THE BODY (PLURAL) _____

Attention, all _____! Santa Claus is looking for
PLURAL NOUN

_____  _____ elves to _____
NUMBER                        ADJECTIVE                                        VERB

in his workshop at the North _____. Job responsibilities
NOUN

include making toy _____ faster than the speed of
PLURAL NOUN

_____; taking care of eight _____ reindeer
NOUN                                                          ADJECTIVE

when necessary; repairing Santa's shiny, red _____; and, of
NOUN

course, sorting letters from _____ girls and boys. Some very
ADJECTIVE

_____ elves might get the chance to _____
ADJECTIVE                                                                  VERB

in Santa's sleigh on Christmas Eve and help him deliver _____
PLURAL NOUN

all over (the) _____. Most importantly, candidates'
A PLACE

_____ must be full of Christmas cheer!
PART OF THE BODY (PLURAL)

MAD LIBS® is fun to play with friends, but you can also play it by yourself! To begin with, DO NOT look at the story on the page below. Fill in the blanks on this page with the words called for. Then, using the words you have selected, fill in the blank spaces in the story.

Now you've created your own hilarious MAD LIBS® game!

# SNOW DAY!

NOUN _____

ADJECTIVE _____

NOUN _____

ADJECTIVE _____

NOUN _____

ADJECTIVE _____

NOUN _____

NOUN _____

NOUN _____

NOUN _____

NOUN _____

VERB _____

ADJECTIVE _____

PLURAL NOUN _____

NOUN _____

# MAD LIBS®

## SNOW DAY!

This is your lucky _____. Because of the _____
            NOUN                                        ADJECTIVE

blizzard, school's been canceled. So how will you spend this unexpected

_____? Here are some _____ suggestions:
    NOUN                              ADJECTIVE

- Stay inside and drink hot _____ while watching _____
                                NOUN                        ADJECTIVE

  cartoons on television.

- Grab your _____ and go sledding down a steep _____.
             NOUN                                    NOUN

- Find a frozen _____ and go ice-skating on it.
                  NOUN

- Build a/an _____ fort. Construct walls out of hard-packed
                 NOUN

  _____, then _____ inside for hours on end.
       NOUN                      VERB

- Break up into _____ teams and have a snowball fight with
                 ADJECTIVE

  your neighborhood _____.
                    PLURAL NOUN

- Sleep the _____ away.
             NOUN

MAD LIBS® is fun to play with friends, but you can also play it by yourself! To begin with, DO NOT look at the story on the page below. Fill in the blanks on this page with the words called for. Then, using the words you have selected, fill in the blank spaces in the story.

Now you've created your own hilarious MAD LIBS® game!

## THE NUTCRACKER

ADJECTIVE _____

NOUN _____

NOUN _____

ADJECTIVE _____

ADJECTIVE _____

NOUN _____

ADJECTIVE _____

PLURAL NOUN _____

ADJECTIVE _____

PLURAL NOUN _____

TYPE OF FOOD _____

TYPE OF LIQUID _____

VERB ENDING IN "ING" _____

ADJECTIVE _____

ADJECTIVE _____

# MAD LIBS®
# THE NUTCRACKER

*The Nutcracker* is a famous ballet that tells the _____ story
<br>ADJECTIVE

of a little _____ named Clara whose godfather gives her a/an
<br>NOUN

_____-cracker for Christmas. Amazingly, the nutcracker comes
<br>NOUN

to life as a/an _____ prince who rescues Clara from some
<br>ADJECTIVE

very _____ mice. Then Clara and her prince travel to a magical
<br>ADJECTIVE

_____, where they are greeted by _____
<br>NOUN      ADJECTIVE

snowflakes and dancing _____. They continue their enchanted
<br>PLURAL NOUN

journey and enter the _____ land of the Sugar Plum
<br>ADJECTIVE

_____, where people dressed like _____ and
<br>PLURAL NOUN      TYPE OF FOOD

_____ dance for them. When the festivities are over, Clara finds
<br>TYPE OF LIQUID

herself at home, _____ under the Christmas tree and holding her
<br>VERB ENDING IN "ING"

_____ nutcracker. It was all just a/an _____ dream!
<br>ADJECTIVE      ADJECTIVE

MAD LIBS® is fun to play with friends, but you can also play it by yourself! To begin with, DO NOT look at the story on the page below. Fill in the blanks on this page with the words called for. Then, using the words you have selected, fill in the blank spaces in the story.

Now you've created your own hilarious MAD LIBS® game!

## SANTA TALKS

NOUN _____

ADJECTIVE _____

NOUN _____

NOUN _____

NOUN _____

PLURAL NOUN _____

NUMBER _____

PLURAL NOUN _____

PART OF THE BODY _____

NOUN _____

ADJECTIVE _____

PLURAL NOUN _____

ADJECTIVE _____

ADJECTIVE _____

ADJECTIVE _____

# MAD LIBS®
# SANTA TALKS

The following is an exclusive interview at the North _____ with
                                                              NOUN

the rotund man in the _____ suit:
                          ADJECTIVE

Q: You are described as a jolly _____. Are you that way 24/7?
                                      NOUN

Santa: Ho, ho, ho. Does that answer your _____?
                                              NOUN

Q: My next _____ may be somewhat embarrassing. Have you put
                NOUN

on some extra _____ recently?
                  PLURAL NOUN

Santa: I'm actually at my average weight of _____ pounds.
                                                  NUMBER

Q: Doesn't that make it difficult for you to get down chimneys, especially

carrying a sack full of children's _____?
                                        PLURAL NOUN

Santa: No, I just suck in my _____ and squeeze down the
                                PART OF THE BODY

_____. I'm sorry—we're going to have to cut this _____
   NOUN                                                          ADJECTIVE

interview short. I've got to get all the kids' _____ delivered by daybreak.
                                                  PLURAL NOUN

Q: Wait—how do you get around the _____ world in one night?
                                        ADJECTIVE

Santa:  I have a/an _____ sleigh and a/an _____
                        ADJECTIVE                        ADJECTIVE

team of reindeer—and remember, most of the world is downhill these days.

Ho, ho, ho!

MAD LIBS® is fun to play with friends, but you can also play it by yourself! To begin with, DO NOT look at the story on the page below. Fill in the blanks on this page with the words called for. Then, using the words you have selected, fill in the blank spaces in the story.

Now you've created your own hilarious MAD LIBS® game!

# CHRISTMAS COOKIES

NOUN _____

NOUN _____

PLURAL NOUN _____

PLURAL NOUN _____

PLURAL NOUN _____

PLURAL NOUN _____

PLURAL NOUN _____

PLURAL NOUN _____

NOUN _____

PLURAL NOUN _____

NOUN _____

ADJECTIVE _____

ADJECTIVE _____

ADVERB _____

ADJECTIVE _____

ADJECTIVE _____

ADJECTIVE _____

# MAD LIBS®
# CHRISTMAS COOKIES

Whether red or green, covered with sprinkles or just plain old _____,
NOUN

Christmas cookies are the _____'s meow! Some of the tastiest of
NOUN

these _____ include:
PLURAL NOUN

• Sugar _____: These rank as one of the most popular Christmas
PLURAL NOUN

_____. They are often shaped like Christmas _____ and
PLURAL NOUN                                                    PLURAL NOUN

_____, with frosting and _____ sprinkled on top.
PLURAL NOUN                          PLURAL NOUN

• _____ macaroons: These coconut _____
NOUN                                          PLURAL NOUN

delight the _____-buds, especially when they've been dipped in
NOUN

rich and _____ chocolate.
ADJECTIVE

• Gingerbread cookies: Who can resist the _____ aroma of these
ADJECTIVE

_____ baked spicy classics? At Christmastime they are usually
ADVERB

cut into the shape of _____ girls and _____
ADJECTIVE                                         ADJECTIVE

boys, and many families also build _____ gingerbread houses.
ADJECTIVE

MAD LIBS® is fun to play with friends, but you can also play it by yourself! To begin with, DO NOT look at the story on the page below. Fill in the blanks on this page with the words called for. Then, using the words you have selected, fill in the blank spaces in the story.

Now you've created your own hilarious MAD LIBS® game!

# HOLIDAY ADVICE COLUMN

PERSON IN ROOM (FEMALE) _____

ADVERB _____

PERSON IN ROOM _____

NOUN _____

NOUN _____

ADJECTIVE _____

NOUN _____

NOUN _____

ADVERB _____

ADJECTIVE _____

A PLACE _____

SAME ADJECTIVE _____

ADJECTIVE _____

A PLACE _____

PART OF THE BODY _____

NOUN _____

A PLACE _____

ADJECTIVE _____

# MAD LIBS®
# HOLIDAY ADVICE COLUMN

Dear Miss _____,
          PERSON IN ROOM (FEMALE)

I _____ need your advice. I have to buy a Christmas
     ADVERB

present for my friend, _____. We've known each
                       PERSON IN ROOM

other since the first day of _____ school, and he/she means the
                             NOUN

_____ to me. So here's my _____ problem—my
     NOUN                             ADJECTIVE

friend already owns every _____ known to man. What do I get for
                          NOUN

the _____ who has everything? _____ yours,
     NOUN                                 ADVERB

_____ in (the) _____
     ADJECTIVE              A PLACE

Dear _____,
      SAME ADJECTIVE

The solution to your _____ dilemma is easy! We're talking about
                     ADJECTIVE

your best friend in all of (the) _____. It doesn't matter what
                                 A PLACE

you give—so long as it comes from the _____. Try making your
                                      PART OF THE BODY

friend a homemade _____, or give him/her a gift certificate
                   NOUN

to (the) _____. No matter what you decide, your friend will
          A PLACE

appreciate the _____ thought.
                ADJECTIVE

MAD LIBS® is fun to play with friends, but you can also play it by yourself! To begin with, DO NOT look at the story on the page below. Fill in the blanks on this page with the words called for. Then, using the words you have selected, fill in the blank spaces in the story.

Now you've created your own hilarious MAD LIBS® game!

---

# A SPECIAL RECIPE FOR HOT CHOCOLATE

ADJECTIVE _____

PART OF THE BODY (PLURAL) _____

PLURAL NOUN _____

ADJECTIVE _____

TYPE OF LIQUID _____

NOUN _____

NOUN _____

ADJECTIVE _____

NUMBER _____

NUMBER _____

ADVERB _____

ADJECTIVE _____

NOUN _____

NOUN _____

ADJECTIVE _____

NOUN _____

# MAD LIBS®
## A SPECIAL RECIPE FOR HOT CHOCOLATE

There is nothing more comforting than a/an _____, frothy
<br>ADJECTIVE

hot chocolate to warm up your _____ on the coldest
<br>PART OF THE BODY (PLURAL)

_____ of winter. Here is a recipe that has been passed down
<br>PLURAL NOUN

from generation to generation in my _____ family. Pour one
<br>ADJECTIVE

cup of _____, one _____ of half-and-half, one
<br>TYPE OF LIQUID               NOUN

tablespoon of vanilla, and two ounces of semisweet _____ into a/an
<br>NOUN

_____ pan. Place it on the stove and heat at _____
<br>ADJECTIVE                              NUMBER

degrees for _____ minutes. Stir _____ until
<br>NUMBER                  ADVERB

the chocolate melts. Pour the liquid into two _____ mugs
<br>ADJECTIVE

and serve with a dollop of whipped _____ on top. If you add
<br>NOUN

some atmosphere, your _____ will taste even better: Enjoy your
<br>NOUN

drink in front of a/an _____ fireplace or while watching the
<br>ADJECTIVE

_____-flakes fall outside your window.
<br>NOUN

MAD LIBS® is fun to play with friends, but you can also play it by yourself! To begin with, DO NOT look at the story on the page below. Fill in the blanks on this page with the words called for. Then, using the words you have selected, fill in the blank spaces in the story.

Now you've created your own hilarious MAD LIBS® game!

# HOW TO MAKE A SNOWMAN

ADJECTIVE _____

PLURAL NOUN _____

ADJECTIVE _____

ADJECTIVE _____

PART OF THE BODY _____

NOUN _____

ADJECTIVE _____

PLURAL NOUN _____

PART OF THE BODY (PLURAL) _____

NOUN _____

PART OF THE BODY _____

NOUN _____

NOUN _____

PLURAL NOUN _____

NOUN _____

ADJECTIVE _____

NOUN _____

# MAD LIBS®
# HOW TO MAKE A SNOWMAN

Want to make a/an _____ snowman? All you need is some
               ADJECTIVE

snow and a few household _____. Then just follow this
                   PLURAL NOUN

_____ step-by-step guide:
   ADJECTIVE

• Roll three _____ balls out of snow: one for the base, one for
            ADJECTIVE

the torso, and one for the _____. Then pile them on top of one
              PART OF THE BODY

another so they resemble a/an _____.
                   NOUN

• To complete your snowman's _____ body, use some long, thin
                  ADJECTIVE

_____ for arms and give him a pair of _____
 PLURAL NOUN                       PART OF THE BODY (PLURAL)

made of coal. Then add a button _____ and a carrot
                    NOUN

_____.
 PART OF THE BODY

• You can accessorize your creation with a corncob _____, a
                        NOUN

stovepipe _____, and some buttons made of _____.
       NOUN                       PLURAL NOUN

If it's really cold outside, you can give him a knitted _____.
                          NOUN

• And don't forget to give your snowman a name! _____ the
                         ADJECTIVE

_____-man is always a popular choice.
   NOUN

MAD LIBS® is fun to play with friends, but you can also play it by yourself! To begin with, DO NOT look at the story on the page below. Fill in the blanks on this page with the words called for. Then, using the words you have selected, fill in the blank spaces in the story.

Now you've created your own hilarious MAD LIBS® game!

# ELF-MAIL

PERSON IN ROOM _____

PERSON IN ROOM _____

ADJECTIVE _____

ADJECTIVE _____

ADJECTIVE _____

PLURAL NOUN _____

ADJECTIVE _____

PERSON IN ROOM _____

NOUN _____

ADJECTIVE _____

ADJECTIVE _____

PERSON IN ROOM _____

NOUN _____

VERB _____

PLURAL NOUN _____

# MAD LIBS®
## ELF-MAIL

To: _____-elf@santasworkshop.elf
     PERSON IN ROOM

From: _____slittlehelper@santasworkshop.elf
     PERSON IN ROOM

Hi there, _____ buddy! Just wanted to drop you
            ADJECTIVE

a/an _____ note to see how you are doing. It's been a/an
     ADJECTIVE

_____ Christmas season here. I've made so many toys—
  ADJECTIVE

especially jack-in-the-_____—that I've lost count! On another
          PLURAL NOUN

_____ note, are you getting excited about _____'s
  ADJECTIVE                      PERSON IN ROOM

Christmas Eve elf party? I hear DJ _____ Elf will be
                         NOUN

spinning some really _____ Christmas tunes! I've also got
           ADJECTIVE

some _____ gossip: I hear _____ is a shoo-
     ADJECTIVE              PERSON IN ROOM

in for Elf of the Year! He/She totally deserves it for being such a hardworking

_____. Well, I've gotta _____—it's back to the
  NOUN                   VERB

_____ at the workshop. See you soon!
  PLURAL NOUN

MAD LIBS® is fun to play with friends, but you can also play it by yourself! To begin with, DO NOT look at the story on the page below. Fill in the blanks on this page with the words called for. Then, using the words you have selected, fill in the blank spaces in the story.

Now you've created your own hilarious MAD LIBS® game!

# A CHRISTMAS CARD

ADJECTIVE _____

ADJECTIVE _____

NOUN _____

NOUN _____

ADJECTIVE _____

PLURAL NOUN _____

PLURAL NOUN _____

ADJECTIVE _____

NOUN _____

ADJECTIVE _____

VERB _____

ADJECTIVE _____

NOUN _____

PLURAL NOUN _____

NOUN _____

NOUN _____

PERSON IN ROOM _____

# MAD LIBS®
# A CHRISTMAS CARD

Dear Grandma and Grandpa,

Merry Christmas to my wonderful, _____ grandparents. Our
                                        ADJECTIVE

house is filled with _____ Christmas spirit. Yesterday, we went to
                            ADJECTIVE

the _____ farm and bought a ten-foot-tall _____.
            NOUN                                                NOUN

We put it in our _____ living room and covered it with lights
                        ADJECTIVE

and _____. Dad decorated the front of the house with strings of
        PLURAL NOUN

_____ and _____ decorations. And Mom baked
    PLURAL NOUN                ADJECTIVE

a lot of _____ cookies that smell absolutely _____!
                NOUN                                                ADJECTIVE

I hope you're excited about coming to _____ with us! I can't
                                                VERB

wait to see you at our _____ Christmas dinner. We're having
                                ADJECTIVE

your favorite—roast _____ and mashed _____!
                            NOUN                            PLURAL NOUN

And, of course, _____ pie for dessert!
                        NOUN

Love from your grand-_____,
                                NOUN

_____
PERSON IN ROOM

# MAD LIBS®

You can collect these other oversize special-edition Mad Libs® at stores near you!

**BEST OF MAD LIBS**

50 YEARS OF PLURAL NOUN MAD LIBS

Over 125 classic Mad Libs stories inside
Top celebrities fill in their own wacky Mad Libs!
Plus, how this famous game got its start!

by Roger Price & Leonard Stern

*More* **BEST OF MAD LIBS**

MAD LIBS®
*World's Greatest Word Game*

Over 140 classic Mad Libs stories inside!

A super silly way to fill in the _____!
(plural noun)

by Roger Price & Leonard Stern